PRO TACTICS™

NORTHERN PIKE

PRO TACTICS™

NORTHERN PIKE

*Use the Secrets of the Pros to
Catch More and Bigger Pike*

Jack Penny

THE LYONS PRESS
Guilford, Connecticut
An imprint of The Globe Pequot Press

Copyright © 2008 Morris Book Publishing LLC

The Lyons Press is an imprint of The Globe Pequot Press.
Pro Tactics is a trademark of Morris Book Publishing, LLC.

Illustrations by Michael Gellatly © Morris Book Publishing, LLC

Text design by Peter Holm, Sterling Hill Productions

Library of Congress Cataloging-in-Publication Data is available.

ISBN 978-1-59921-257-9

Printed in the United States of America

10 9 8 7 6 5 4 3 2 1

CONTENTS

Acknowledgments | vii

Introduction   **The Great Northern Pike** | 1

Chapter One   **Seasonal Movements** | 5

Chapter Two   **Preservation of the Species** | 7
Equipment • The Landing Method • Removing the Hooks • The Release • Reproduction Mounts • Tips on Taking a Good Photo

Chapter Three   **Proper Tools for the Job at Hand** | 21
Rods and Reels • Other Essential Tools • Leaders

Chapter Four   **Ice-Out** | 40
Quick-Strike Rigs • Bait • Considerations When Using Quick-Strike Rigs • Locations in Lakes • Locations in Rivers

Chapter Five   **Spring** | 49
Locations in Lakes • Locations in Rivers • Dams and Dens

Chapter Six   **Summer** | 63
Locations in Lakes: Bays • Points • Weeds • Open Water • Locations in Rivers

Chapter Seven   **Fall** | 77
Locations in Lakes • Locations in Rivers

Chapter Eight   **Winter** | 85
The Hardwater Season • Equipment • Winter Pike Location • Strategies and Tactics • A Possible Winter Alternative

Chapter Nine   **Lure Modifications** | 101
Spoon Modifications • Rattles • Glowing Lures

Chapter Ten   **Throwback Lures** | 107

Chapter Eleven   **Table Fare** | 112
How to Fillet a Northern Pike • Removing the Y-Bones • Frying Pike

Chapter Twelve   **Education** | 123

Index | 125

About the Author | 128

ACKNOWLEDGMENTS

There are so many people to thank for their help with the making of this book, both directly and indirectly, that I could never get them all in here. The ones listed here are those who have made huge contributions and have become valued friends. I thank you all.

First and foremost is my wife and fishing partner, Mary. It has been a crazy ride, Mare. Thanks. And my daughter, Janelle, who never held it against her dad for being gone so much while chasing these great fish and for her excellent help in editing this book. You make your dad proud, Nell.

And to my dad, Ward Penny, who took the time to get the fishing bug installed and firmly in place in me. We'll fish together again someday.

Bob Schutty and Frank Cox, who took me under their wings and took me fishing as a kid after Dad passed away. Thanks for your time and efforts. You made a huge difference.

And to my good friend, Jack Burns, who gave me my first break in this business and who has not only encouraged me, but has helped open many doors. I've learned a lot from Jack, and even at my advancing age, he has helped me to change the way I think about certain aspects of fishing. Thanks for turning me on to my first muskie too, Jack, along with everything else.

Three guys with whom I fished who not only taught me things but also served as inspirations: Al Lindner, Larry Dahlberg, and Bill Tenney.

Pete, Dave, Teresa, Rob, Mel, Trish, and all the staff at *Esox Angler* magazine. I couldn't do all this stuff without you.

And Doug Stange and the staff at *In-Fisherman* who taught me so many things as I was pursuing this pike obsession. Thanks a million. I'm still learning from you guys.

My friend and fellow 'luce nut, Joe Bednar, who has always encouraged me in my writing and who is largely responsible for the ice fishing content in this book.

Ken Bear, who was there from the start and joined me in this pike addiction. One of the best friends I've ever had.

To the whole Wilson clan in Ontario, who have helped me in so many ways over the years.

To Donny Ingle and Darin Gulling, who have both shared many adventures with me in the north country. And Ned Smead, my old fishing partner. Rest in peace, my good friend.

Many thanks to Mike Trettin for his help with some of the photographs in this book.

And to all the guides, outfitters, and fishermen I've fished with over the years. There are too many to name, but you know who you are. I learned from all of you, and I thank you.

And last, but surely not least, Chad and Tanya Fortner of Nungesser Lake Lodge, who have become close friends and have put up with me for the last ten years at ice-out time.

The Great Northern Pike

Why pike? I can't count the number of times that question has been put to me. There are several reasons why I choose pike. I love a pike's aggressive nature and its willingness to attack. And I love the challenge that catching a true trophy presents. And the wilderness settings in which pike reside are very close to my heart.

And what about you, the reader of this book? Maybe you are a bass or walleye angler looking to catch something that could eat most of the fish you normally catch. You could be someone who works hard and wants to learn how to make the most out of your free time. Or perhaps you want to take the family on a vacation and have those kids catch fish until their arms are sore. Or take your wife to a special hideaway and have her experience firsthand what makes you a fish nut. Whatever your reason, pike are a great candidate to fulfill it, and I hope that I can help make your efforts successful.

My intent in writing this book is to help you learn how to catch more and bigger northern pike by sharing what I have learned over the past thirty-plus years. As you read through the book, I will take you through the entire season, from ice-out through the freeze-up, and explain where

Few other freshwater fish offer the combination of aggressiveness, fight, and size as northern pike. MARY PENNY

to fish, what to use, and how to use it. I'll show you different techniques and tricks I've learned over the last three decades. I'll show you how to make better leaders than you can buy—and that will cost you less—and how to modify certain lures to make them more effective. And I will explain the importance of catch-and-release fishing and how to successfully complete this process.

Fishermen and women have different thoughts on what makes a successful outing on the water. Some enjoy just catching a lot of fish. Others are content to work hard for just one big fish. There is no right or wrong in all this; it is a matter of personal preference. As for me, I just like catching pike and consider the trip successful when I do. In this book, I will attempt to help everyone make their outings more successful. I will point you to locations that are high-percentage spots for trophy-size pike. In fishing most of these big-fish locations, you will no doubt rack up some numbers at the same time, although a couple of them will be exclusively big fish spots. In pike fishing, it is normal to weed through smaller and midsize fish to catch big ones.

How It All Began

I have been asked in the past how I learned so much about these pike. There are several answers to this question. I caught my first pike in the late 1950s and can remember being very excited. The fish was small, but in the eyes of a six-year-old kid it was huge. On that same family vacation, my dad later caught one that weighed in at seventeen pounds on his old De-Liar scale. I couldn't believe the size of that monster, and it elevated Dad to a status far above any of my other heroes of the time. The seed had been planted. Later in life, after I was grown and had a job, I took a trip to Kississing Lake in Manitoba with some co-workers. It was during this trip that the seed, planted so many years before, sprouted and grew into an obsession that is still alive today.

So I started to study these great fish. I read everything I could find that had anything to do with pike, and faithfully watched all the fishing shows hoping for more pike information. I was a student and took it very seriously. I met my wife-to-be in the mid-70s, and took her on a trip to that same lake, Kississing, and to my surprise, she caught the bug too. That was all it took. I married that girl and we've been a pike-fishing team ever since. Over the years, Mary and I have shared both successes and disappointments together. We saved our money and began taking trips, starting in the northern United States, and progressively worked our way further north, all the way to the Arctic Circle. Along the way, we met others who fished for pike, and listened intently to what they had to say. If we had a guide, we filled his day with questions. The whole idea was to learn something from every pike fisherman we encountered.

We have caught a good number of trophy pike over the years, and met so many characters, it would be tough to put a number to them. There have been some tense and dangerous moments, like the time we faced an Alaskan grizzly bear from a mere seven yards. And we've seen things that would make you laugh out loud, like witnessing a seagull and a mink fight it out over a dead fish. Yes, we've made a lot of great memories over the years, and it is not over yet. There is just too much fun to be had, in this pursuit of the great northern pike, to quit.

Eventually, our education started to pay off, and it showed in our catches. We caught more and bigger fish with much greater frequency. For a while, we compared our catches with those in the record books, and realized we were contenders for many of the categories listed, so we went a bit crazy trying to get our names listed in there. Before it was over, I had eight line-class records and Mary had three, which included the all-tackle blue/silver pike that, at the time of this writing, is still on top. All of these records were awarded to us by the National Freshwater Fishing Hall of Fame in Hayward, Wisconsin.

The best education we received, however, was on the water. And we spent every hour we could there. *In-Fisherman* magazine and others provided us with the ideas, but we had to learn to apply them ourselves. While this took time, it wasn't long before we started putting the pieces of the puzzle together and our catch rates skyrocketed. The learning process didn't stop there, though. We are still students learning from these great fish.

In this book you will see references to specific products. I want the reader to know that I am not on anybody's payroll and am not paid to recommend any of the products mentioned. I have chased these pike for a long time, and have tried almost everything I saw that I thought had even a remote chance of being successful. Anything you see in this book is what I have settled on as being the best for my purposes. In some instances, you may already have certain tools, which differ from those I use, that you feel work best for you. And this is fine. I still try new products every year, and occasionally find something to add to my arsenal. I encourage you to keep an open mind as well.

CHAPTER ONE

Seasonal Movements

Large pike are creatures of seasonal movements. In other words, in a given body of water, where you find them in June is not where you'll find them in July. The seasonal locations of these fish cannot be predicted by the calendar hanging on your wall. They instead follow a calendar set by nature.

Water temperature will dictate when seasonal movements are made and where big pike are located. It is for this reason that I do not attempt to relate these locations and movements to you based on calendar periods, but instead will use temperature ranges to point you in the right direction. It is important to keep in mind that not all pike in a given system make their movements at exactly the same temperature. Do not think that the day the water hits 65 degrees, all the big pike leave the shallows. Rather, by the time the temperature reaches 65 degrees, the big pike will have vacated the shallows. Some may leave at 55 degrees, some at 60 degrees, while others may wait until it is 62 degrees. It is a matter of temperature ranges, and these ranges have an inaccuracy to them of at least a few degrees. In each section of this book when there is movement involved, I will list temperature ranges that correspond with these movements.

In some cases, seasonal changes can put pike off the bite for a while. There are two things that have the most dramatic effect on pike behavior: the weather and the fish's environment. If either one goes through rapid changes, pike will need an adjustment period and will be tough to catch during this time.

CHAPTER TWO

Preservation
of the Species

Before we get into the fishing, let's look at something of great importance—the welfare of these great northern pike. The attitude toward catch-and-release fishing has come a long way since its inception. The benefits have become obvious even to those who scoffed at the idea in the beginning, and it is easy to see why. In many places, fishing is better than it has ever been.

Unfortunately, not all fishermen and women are on board with catch and release. There are still those that kill big pike, be it for a wall ornament or for food. I hate to think of all the huge pike that are still sitting in someone's freezer, getting frostbitten, and never even making it to the taxidermist. And there are plenty of well-intentioned fisherfolk who do release big fish that never survive because of improper handling.

Now, I'm not trying to come off as "holier than thou" here. I've made more than my share of mistakes. You'll see evidence of that in this book—namely, the photos sporting vertical holds. Please keep in mind, these photos are several years old. We never hold out catches in this manner anymore because we've learned that it is harmful to the pike. The internal organs must be supported, and now we only use a horizontal hold, if we pick them up at all. This has been a long learning process, but I like to think we're much easier on the fish now than we were back then, even though our intentions were good then as well. Just because you put a fish back in the water, and it swims away, does not mean it survived. Some will swim to the bottom, turn on their sides, and die. It's just delayed mortality. I hate thinking about the big pike we undoubtedly damaged, but we learned. I relate these mistakes we've made in the hope that you will not make the same mistakes.

Most of the time, you won't know if the fish lives or not, but there are certain steps you can take that will greatly increase their chances, and make you reasonably certain they lived through the encounter. Remember, catch and release is effective only if the fish survives.

Equipment

First, let's take a look at the tools for this job. The first thing we'll need is a landing device. The best is a cradle or a net, or a cross between the two called a Kwik Kradle. I am not a believer in those jaw-gripping tools still available. There is too much chance of damage to the fish, and hoisting up a big fish supported by the end of its jawbone is out of the question. Our goal here is to avoid injuring the fish. For many years I hand-landed all of our bigger fish, and thought that was the best way to protect them. I learned that it wasn't, and changed my ways accordingly.

A cradle works well, and there are many who prefer them. They will contain and control the pike for unhooking while keeping it in the water, and they are very fish-friendly. There are cradles with a strap attached, to aid in weighing the fish while it remains contained for those who want to know the weight, and some come with measured markings for determining the fish's length. The best cradles will have one end closed off with netting to prevent the pike from swimming clear through the cradle.

The primary disadvantage is that they are not exactly easy to operate. If you are fishing by yourself, it is nearly impossible. And a child who is handling the landing duties would probably find it very difficult. For the traveling fisherman, the cradle enjoys one distinct advantage in that it is possible to travel with it on airplanes. Rolled up, it will fit into a large rod tube along with some rods. I can't imagine going through airport security with a huge net. I have enough trouble as it is without trying that. Another advantage to using a cradle is its size. If I'm in my boat, I use the Kwik Kradle or a net. But if I'm in a smaller boat or traveling, I take the cradle.

My personal preference is a long-handled net. And not just any net. Those nets made of what looks like twine or heavy cord with knots in the mesh are not going to do pike any favors. They damage the fins and remove some of the slime coat. This will certainly cause a bacterial infection, which ultimately results in death.

The best nets feature a coating on the mesh that looks like hard rubber, and have no knots in the mesh. One great feature of this mesh material is that it is nearly impossible for a hook to penetrate, meaning no more tangled lures. Also, it will not remove any of the pike's slime coat. Look for a net that has an extra-large hoop opening, at least thirty inches in diameter. An extra-deep bag is also very important, as I'll explain below.

I like and use nets made by Frabill. To my knowledge, they were the first ones to offer coated, knotless netting to help preserve fish. They have also reintroduced their Kwik Kradle, a great net/cradle hybrid.

Reviving one after landing. Notice the absence of knots in the net's mesh. PETE MAINA

The Landing Method

There are a couple of critical errors, which can lead to a lost fish, that the inexperienced angler may make. First, do not reel in all your line while bringing the pike boatside. More pike are lost at the boat than anywhere else. Pike, especially big ones, are notorious for making a last-ditch effort to escape with a huge burst of energy at the last moment. When the pike is approaching, leave out about the same amount of line as the length of your rod. That way, if the pike lunges, you'll have some cushion to absorb the shock to the line and hook.

Another time a lot of pike become unhooked is when the pike is being pulled toward the boat at the end of the fight. After a fierce battle, hooks are not embedded as well as they were at the initial hookup. Instead of attempting to guide the pike into the landing device by raising the rod tip, it is much better to just hold the tip high but stationary, and take a couple of steps backwards. The pike will glide right in. Of course, you must make sure there is nothing behind you to trip over, and make sure you don't fall over the side. In some boats, there just isn't room for this; in that case, you have to go back to the regular routine.

Okay, your partner has a huge pike at boatside. If you're using a cradle, you're leaning over the side of the boat with the cradle open, holding it by the frame on both sides, with the leading end of it in the water. The angler steers the pike (head-first) toward you, and as soon as the fish clears

A big pike entering the cradle.
JACK PENNY

the netting and is fully inside the cradle, you quickly close the opening, lift slightly to enclose the fish in the mesh while continuing to keep it in the water, and you've succeeded. Keep the pike suspended in the water while you get ready to unhook it or while your photographer gets ready.

The net or Kwik Kradle requires a different technique. Place one hand a foot or more back from the hoop, wherever it is most comfortable. (I'm right-handed, so this would be my left hand.) Place the other hand closer to the end of the handle. Because the bag of the net is so deep, you'll find it easiest to grasp the bottom of the bag in your hand closest to the hoop (the Kwik Kradle doesn't require this), thereby avoiding getting it snagged on something in the boat. As the angler guides the fish toward you, dip the leading edge of the net in the water. As the fish enters the net, release the netting bag from your leading hand, and scoop up the fish with one fluid motion. Raise the net high enough to prevent escape, and she's now a caught fish. Remember only to net the fish head-first. If you attempt to net a big pike tail-first, she will thrust forward and possibly become unhooked and escape, leaving you with— at the very least—a disappointed angler.

Look closely to determine the location of the hooks before attempting to remove them.
MARY PENNY

Removing the Hooks

The unhooking process is a two-man job, either with a net or with the cradle. One person holds the landing device while the other takes care of unhooking the fish. With the net, hold it high up enough that the fish won't jump out, and low enough so the hook man can do his job while the fish is still in the water. Essentially, the net now becomes a holding pen, containing the pike for the unhooking process.

Our next chore is unhooking the fish. You want to complete this process as quickly as possible for the sake of the pike. There are three possible tools you might need: a long needle-nose pliers, a hook cutter like a Knipex, and possibly a jaw spreader. Keep these tools in a place where

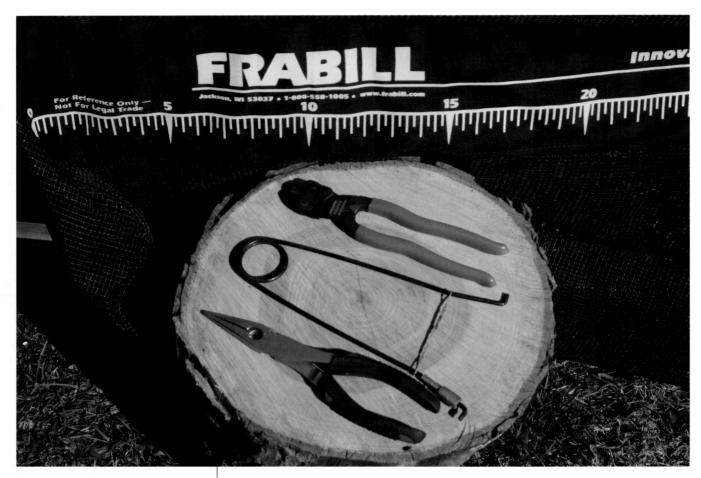

Unhooking a fish properly requires the right tools. Shown here are needle-nose pliers, jaw spreaders, and Knipex hook cutters. JACK PENNY

they are easily accessible, so you can complete this process as quickly as possible.

The first thing to do is to look at the fish and determine where it is hooked. In the best-case scenario, the fish will be hooked where you can grab the hook with the pliers and remove it while the fish remains in the water. If the hook or hooks are not visible and are inside the mouth, you will need to take a hold of the fish. Always wet your hands before grabbing a pike, to prevent slime removal. If the pike isn't too wide across the back, you may be able to grab it behind the head, just behind the gill flaps. Applying slight pressure will temporarily paralyze the pike. If the fish is too wide to grab behind the head, you'll have to apply the jaw hold. This can be intimidating to the uninitiated, but it is not that difficult and after a few times becomes second nature.

First, grab the fish on the opposite side from the hooks. If the pike is hooked on the right side of its mouth, reach down on the left side with your left hand, curve your fingers inward, and start sliding them along

The jaw hold on a large pike. Notice the placement of the thumb and fingers. MARY PENNY

and up into the gill flap. Care must be taken here to avoid the red gill filaments, but with your fingers curved in and by slightly pulling out on the gill flap, you should miss them. Should you come into contact with these gill filaments, you will surely know it immediately. They will stick to your fingers like Velcro and when you pull away, you will leave some skin behind. Slide your hand all the way forward, with curved fingers in and your thumb outside the fish, until you reach the end of the flap opening. When you reach the end, grasp the flap (actually, there is a jawbone located here), and tighten your grip with curved fingers inside and your thumb on the membranelike skin on the outside, gripping the jawbone. This is no time to be timid. When you grab her, grip her tightly.

You can now pick up the head and look inside the mouth to see how deeply the fish is hooked. If the pike is being stubborn and won't open its mouth, jaw spreaders will open it so you can safely pry the hooks out. If the hooks are too deep, either cut them with the hook cutters, or possibly go in the back door through the gill flaps and attempt to pull the lure out

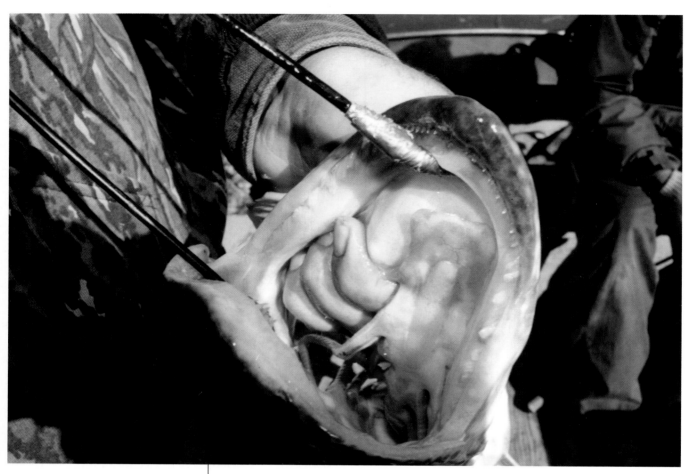

Use jaw spreaders to keep the fish's mouth open. Note how the holder's fingers are curled and away from the gill filaments.
MARY PENNY

through the flap and cut your line, leaving the lure and leader outside the fish, and pull your line back out through the mouth. However, this should only be done as a last resort.

For the sake of the pike, hook cutters are the recommended method, and Knipex cutters will easily cut the strongest hooks. After cutting the hooks below the barb, it is best to go back with the pliers and attempt to remove the hook points. Most will fall out anyway, but why leave the fish with hook points in it? If it is not possible to get the points out easily, leave them in. Better that than risk further damage to tissue, or have the head out of the water too long.

Now that you have the pike unhooked, it is time for a decision. Most people will want a picture of the fish, and that's fine as long as you do it correctly. Have the photographer get into position while the fish remains in the water, and focus the camera before picking up the fish. Keep in mind that the head must remain in the water so the pike can breathe. Using the jaw hold with wet hands, pick the head up and use the other hand to support the midsection of the fish so you are supporting those internal organs. Turn toward the photographer and let him or her take a couple of quick shots. Then immediately place the pike back in the cradle or net. If you require more photos, let the pike catch its breath before picking it up again.

If you feel you must weigh the fish, please do not hang it vertically from a scale. Europeans use what is called a weigh sack. This product is lined with a rubberized material that, when wet, will not remove slime. It also fully supports the pike, and comes with straps attached to hang it from a scale. If you don't have a cradle suitable for weighing, look for a weigh sack. They are often found on eBay.

The Release

As soon as you have taken pictures and have the weight (if these are desired), it is time to revive the fish. Keep in mind that the warmer the water is, the more a pike will be stressed from the fight and the longer it will take to revive it. A common mistake here is to move the fish back and forth in the water. This is not good for the pike, as it is completely unnatural for them to move backwards. Too much backward movement can actually drown a pike. It is far better to let the fish lie stationary while holding on and supporting its midsection with both hands. After it lies motionless for a while, you should feel it start to tense up. This is a sign that the fish is recovering and is nearly ready to go. Slowly move the fish forward, and reach back and give its tail a slight squeeze.

If the fish is ready when you squeeze the tail, it will take off. If it doesn't, bring it back and resume holding it motionless. While you are holding it stationary with both hands near the midsection, it is sometimes possible to hasten recovery by

Supporting the midsection of a big pike while holding it motionless is much better than moving it back and forth.
MARY PENNY

As the fish appears to be ready to go, reach back and give the tail a gentle but firm squeeze.
MARY PENNY

curling your fingers up, slightly depressing the stomach area, and while keeping the fish motionless, moving your hands forward and back in a sort of massaging maneuver. (This is a great time, by the way, to capture a release photo.) When the fish makes its break for freedom, congratulate yourself and your partner. You both deserve it—you not only caught a trophy pike, but you also did your part in preserving the species. I absolutely love watching a big fish swim away. The process usually takes five minutes or less, but I have held pike for twenty minutes and longer, especially when the water is warmer.

Reproduction Mounts

I'm sure there are some thinking, "Hey, that is fine and dandy, but I want a mount on the wall." Fear not; you can still have that trophy. Nowadays there are reproduction mounts available that look as good as, or better than, a skin

A vigorous splash as the fish departs is often a good sign that it will survive its ordeal.
MARY PENNY

mount, and the fact that they will last indefinitely, as opposed to about twenty years for a skin mount, makes them a much better choice. Your grandkids will be able to brag, "My grandpa caught that fish back in '08."

I know of two major players in the reproduction mount game. Again, there may be more, but these are the ones I know do excellent work.

Lax Reproductions. Rick Lax has been working in his father's taxidermy shop since he was a small child, learning every phase of this art. Somewhere along the line, Ron and Rick Lax figured that with the high numbers of huge fish they were entrusted to mount, they ought to do something to help preserve these species, and that is where their reproduction business started. They started making molds of all the big fish that came into their shop, and eventually started offering replica mounts for sale. Ron Lax retired in 2003, and son Rick took over the business. Rick Lax Reproductions is located in Conover, Wisconsin, and can be contacted at 715-547-3710. Alternately, they can be reached through the Internet at www.laxreproductions.com.

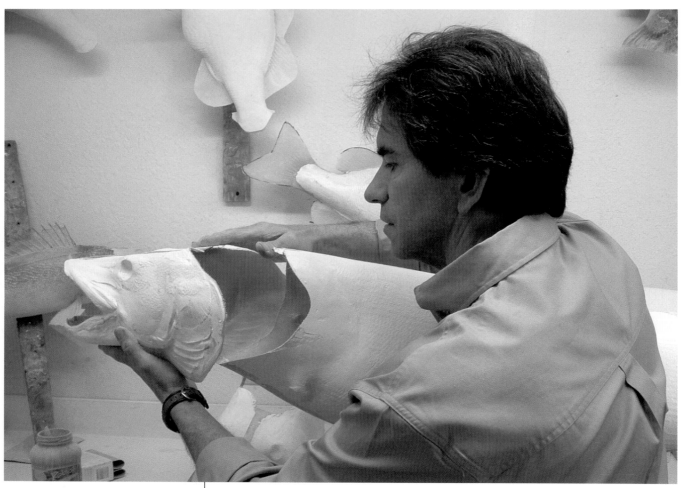

Joe Fittante fits the head on a replica pike form. JOE FITTANTE

Fittante Replicas. Joe Fittante started in the taxidermy business around 1971. As a youngster, Joe had an interest in art and fishing, and when he was old enough, he approached the best taxidermist he knew and asked if he could serve as an apprentice in order to learn this art. Years later, after branching out on his own, Joe decided sometime around the mid-80s that with the new catch-and-release philosophy he had to change directions. This led him to producing replica mounts. Joe went on to become one of the very best in his chosen field and has won many awards for his work. Fittante Replicas can be reached at (715) 627-7662 or toll free at (800) 261-2327. His Web site is www.fittantereplicas.com. You can also e-mail Joe at info@fittantereplicas.com.

All you need is a photograph of the fish and the measurements. And if you're not too picky, a photograph is not mandatory. But with a good photo, either of these guys can make your mount look exactly like the fish you released.

Tips on Taking a Good Photo

While I am on the subject of photographs, I think it is best to include a few tips for top-quality pictures. First, always have the sun shining on the photographer's back and the angler's front. To do otherwise will only produce washed-out photos. Next, always use a flash. That cap that the subject is wearing shades the face, and sometimes you won't even be able to make out who it is. Using a flash will eliminate most of this shadow. The best fish pictures feature the fisherman and the fish, and little else. You want just a little extra space over the top of the head and a little below the fish. Everything else is just clutter. A bit of shoreline background is good, but clutter in the boat only distracts from the angler and the fish. Just be sure when you look through the camera's viewfinder that there is a little extra all the way around the fish and the fisherman, but no more than a few inches. Also, look to be sure that no shadow from the cameraman is showing on the subject.

We've used 35mm cameras for many years, and for the last few years we've been experimenting with digitals. A camera with a wide-angle lens works best, and I prefer a 28mm lens for fish photos inside of the boat. We have found that with a 28mm lens, if the photographer and the angler can both reach out and touch fingertips, they are about the correct distance apart for a pike of about 45 inches.

A big pike . . . that would look better without the photographer's shadow.
MARY PENNY

I have good reason for discussing pike-care techniques to the length that I have. I have witnessed the destruction of great pike water within just a few seasons of hard fishing, and I've seen it much more than once.

It is a matter of genetics, plain and simple. A natural lake will have just so many big predators in it. And the higher up the food chain a species gets, the fewer of them there will be. In the waters where they live, pike are at or very near the top. So, naturally, there are fewer of them. Once they are removed or killed, it takes quite a while for the next contender to grow big enough to replace its older sister. If this happens continually, the upcoming year class won't be able to keep up. Soon that year class will be getting whittled down, too. It doesn't take many years of this before there are nothing but small fish in the system. The gene pool has been depleted, and might never recover. Think of it this way: Fish are like people. When two humans of large stature mate, their offspring will have the potential to grow large also. The same goes for people of a small stature. It would be rare for two healthy people who are five feet tall to produce offspring that would grow to be six feet tall. It is much the same for pike. Big pike produce big pike. Small pike produce small pike. It is the way of nature.

CHAPTER THREE

Proper Tools for the Job at Hand

In this chapter we will cover some of the equipment you will need, including rods, reels, lines, tools, and terminal tackle. Similar to my remarks in the opening chapter, you may already have some of these tools that you prefer to use. The ones featured here are what I have settled on after much experimentation.

Using the correct equipment is important to maximize one's success. Think of it this way: You can back out a screw with a butter knife, but a screwdriver works much better. Both tools will do the job, but one is far and away a better choice. It is much the same with fishing. When you are fishing for pike, don't try it with a crappie outfit.

Rods and Reels

Let's start with the conventional rod-and-reel combinations. Basically, there are two types to consider: spinning and casting. Spincasting gear may work for very small pike, but I wouldn't go looking for a trophy armed with it. Fly-fishing equipment works very well in the hands of those who have knowledge of this type of fishing, but we will not be discussing it in this book.

When you are selecting a rod and reel for pike fishing, there are a couple of considerations to be made. First and foremost, it has to be comfortable for you. The rod has to have enough backbone to get the hooks set in a bony mouth, and it has to be able to cast a variety of lures.

When I refer to the backbone in a rod, I am talking about its strength. Pike come equipped with a mouth full of sharp teeth, and you need a rod that is strong enough to drag a lure through those teeth and still have the strength to bury the hooks in a bony mouth. A rod with too much flex cannot accomplish this. Nearly all rods are rated and marked with the different actions and recommended line and/or lure weights. For example, my jerkbait rod is rated as heavy action for lure weights ranging from 2 to 10 ounces, while my spoon rod is rated as medium-heavy action and is recommended for lures weighing from ¾ to 3 ounces. When you are shopping for a rod, these are good guidelines to follow.

Spinning Gear

Let's start with spinning gear. Spinning gear has its advantages in some situations, and for many it is easier to master. As you get further in this book, you will see that I use spinning gear sparingly. But it will work in most of the situations I will present. However, remember the butter knife analogy. Most of the time I use spinning gear when I'm casting lighter-weight lures and jigs, as I find it easier to get distance in my casts with the open-faced reel. Another situation is jigging in rivers. It is the best tool for the job in these situations.

My spinning outfit includes a walleye-size reel spooled with Cortland's Master Braid in 20-pound test. I have used Berkley's Fireline in the past and liked it also. I'd imagine there are some reading this and are asking themselves, "Why a walleye reel?" I like it because it is small and easy to handle, plus the rod and reel both pack easily for traveling. This is a real plus for me. I only use this gear about 10 percent of the time and have never experienced a failure with it. Walleye rods, however, would be a poor choice. Pike fishing requires a rod with serious backbone while retaining some flex in the upper end. My spinning rod is a two-piece 7-foot rod, rated for lures up to 1½ ounce. While it works well casting lures up to that weight, it also excels at casting lures down to ¼ ounce if needed.

It wasn't many years ago that I would never have considered using a two-piece rod. I tried one when I first started this pursuit of pike, back before graphite rods came along, and didn't care for it. But that was thirty years ago, and like most things these days, rod technology has come a long way. A few years back on a Canadian pike trip, a friend of mine showed me a new rod that he wanted me to try it out. It was a two-piece rod and I didn't expect much, but I fished with it for a while to appease my friend. During my trial run, I hooked and landed a huge pike. The rod performed very well and actually felt good. Not being one to argue with success, I started looking into two-piece rods.

The main advantage for me is the ease of air travel. The major airlines always gave us dirty looks when we showed up with rod cases over seven feet long, but they always took them. The biggest problem was with charter and floatplanes. These smaller aircraft often just couldn't accommodate such a long rod box. I've had to take the rods out of the box and leave it behind while flying with unprotected rods, resulting in broken rods. I've had my rod box strapped to the floats on a floatplane, which meant at least a half gallon of water ended up in the box. The two-piece rods pack into the now-shortened box so much better, and I don't feel like the performance of my rods has suffered at all. Also, I can fit more rods in the box now, and at times, Mary and I can get both of our rods in one box.

Casting Gear

Casting gear gets a bit more complicated than spinning gear. This is due to the fact that, as far as I know, there is no one rod that will do it all. For instance, a rod that I use for casting small spoons is not going to do a good job working jerkbaits. And the rod I use for jerkbaits is not going to troll very well. The idea here is to use the right tool for the job at hand. Keep in mind, though, that some rods will serve nicely for more than one purpose.

When I am selecting rods, I want one with plenty of backbone while retaining an extra-flexible tip. And I also want something I can cast a long way. There are times when covering a lot of water has distinct advantages, like fishing in clear water. If you can see a big pike lying in the shallows, you can bet it can see you too. But if you move off a bit and make long casts, that fish is vulnerable.

Remember that different rod and reels will excel in different situations. For example, if I'm casting spoons in a bay where long casts are not essential,

I'll pick a shorter rod and couple it with a reel that has a slower gear ratio. My choice is a Pete Maina rod that is 6½ feet long, is a two-piece rod, and is rated for lures in the ¾-ounce to 3-ounce range. I couple it with Pete's reel with a 4.3:1 gear ratio and spool 35-pound Cortland Spectron on it. Or let's say I'm casting a big soft-plastic topwater frog through reeds and want to make long casts. I'll pick up my 8½-foot rod and use the faster reel with a 5.2:1 ratio and spooled with the same line. This is probably my best multipurpose rod.

You will no doubt notice that I advocate the use of heavy line, much heavier than one might think necessary. The reason for this is actually simple. It should be apparent by now that I am concerned with the welfare of pike to be released. Pike that fight for an extended period of time build up what is known as lactic acid. If lactic acid concentrations get too high, the pike will certainly die. It is because of this fact that I use heavier lines, which enable me to bring the pike to the boat more quickly and therefore cause it to suffer less lactic-acid buildup. Pike are not "line shy," and you won't miss much by using heavier lines. Plus, with today's "superlines," the diameter is so much smaller that you can use 35-pound line that has the same diameter as 14-pound monofilament line.

For trolling, a longer rod is required. Again, plenty of backbone is needed, and the flexible tip is probably most important with this rod. I use superlines exclusively, and since these are no-stretch lines, I need that tip to serve as a cushion. Without this cushion, the hooks will tear out of the pikes' mouths. For this application, I use a different Pete Maina combo. This one is the same 8½- footer and I use the slower-speed reel but spool it with 50-pound Cortland line. A new 9-foot model was just released, and it is a great trolling rod.

Many of the jerkbaits I use are heavy lures, weighing somewhere between 3 and 5 ounces. Therefore, the heaviest-action rods in my arsenal are reserved for them. Actually, I use two different rods. If I'm traveling by air, I use Pete's 7½-foot two-piece jerkbait rod, rated for lures in the 2- to 10-ounce range. But if I'm in my boat or traveling to a drive- or boat-in destination, I prefer Pete's 8-foot telescoping rod. Both rods are rated for up to 10-ounce lures. You need a faster-speed reel to properly work jerkbaits to pick up the slack line faster between jerks. For line, 50-pound line is the lightest I will consider for jerkbaits, and sometimes I use heavier. In addition to the welfare of the fish, as mentioned above, the reason for heavy line while fishing jerkbaits is not only the weight of the lure, it is also in the way one maneuvers the lure. Jerkbaits have no action of their own and must be manipulated by the angler. This is done by sharply jerking downward with the rod, retrieving most of the slack line, and jerking down again. A small amount of slack must be present when jerking, and this creates tremendous pressure on the line and knot, hence the heavier line.

For larger in-line spinners, spinnerbaits, swimbaits, and smaller crankbaits, I use the same rods I use for spoons, but I switch reels to a faster gear ratio, to reach the faster retrieve speeds needed to use these baits effectively.

So, what brands of rods do I use? My spinning rod came from Cabela's. It is called the Fish Eagle II and is one great rod. I use the spinning gear to cast lightweight topwater lures, small in-line spinners, and lighter jigs. My casting rods, and there are several, are from Bass Pro Shops and are the Pete Maina Signature Series Rods. These are also great rods and are among the best I've ever used, which includes some expensive custom-made rods. They are surprisingly affordable, too. With most things, I've found that you get what you pay for, but these Maina outfits are the exception to that rule. In the end, however, it will be up to you to decide what best serves your purposes.

Reels are another matter. It is my opinion that you need at least two, with different gear ratios. One needs to have a slower retrieval rate than the other. Some lures, like spoons, are more effective when retrieved more

The author's rod-and-reel combinations, from left to right: 9-foot, two-piece trolling rod with a Li'l Ernie; 7½-foot, two-piece jerkbait rod with a Magic Maker; 8½-foot, two-piece casting rod with marabou Mepps; 6½-foot casting rod with a skirted spoon; 7-foot, two-piece spinning rod with lightweight topwater prop-bait.
JACK PENNY

slowly. Others, like jerkbaits or large spinners, require a faster retrieval rate. I got my reels in a combo deal with the rods. The Pete Maina Signature Series combos from Bass Pro Shops were affordable enough that I could outfit myself with several for the price of just one or two of the rods I used to use.

Other Essential Tools

Hook Files

There is another tool that I consider important to success: a hook hone or file. With properly sharpened hooks, your catch rate will soar above the number you will catch with unsharpened hooks. Very few hooks are sharp enough straight out of the package, and this includes most of the new chemically sharpened hooks. If I try to penetrate my thumbnail with a hook and it slides across the nail instead, it is not sharp enough. If it instead digs into the nail, it is ready to go to work. For most top fishermen I know, there are only two hook sharpeners to consider—the hook file and the hard-carbon rods sharpener.

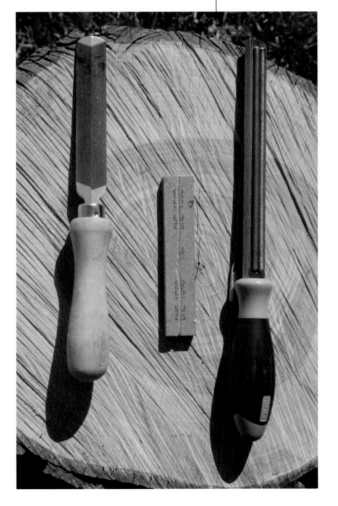

File, stone, and hard carbon sharpener for keeping hooks sharp. JACK PENNY

As with most rules, there are exceptions. To sharpen lighter wire jigs I'll either use a diamond-coated fingernail file or a 150-grit stone into which I cut a groove. Bringing a hook to proper sharpness is not as difficult as one might think, and after a few tries, it will become routine.

With the file, which is what I use most, it is simply a matter of making several angled strokes on one side of the point, then several more on the opposite side, while attempting to duplicate the same angle. After that, make a few strokes across the top of the point. Make all strokes from the back toward the front of the point. With the hard-carbon rods and the stone, all that is required is to set the hook between the rods or the groove in the stone and give it several quick back-and-forth strokes.

Always keep one of these tools handy during fishing, and use it as often as needed. Once a hook has been sharpened initially, it just takes a couple of strokes to bring it back to needle-sharpness. Sharp hooks are essential, and paying attention to these little details will add up to a lot more landed pike in the end.

Electronics

Using good electronics has become a way of life in modern pike fishing. A good depth finder is vital to certain aspects of pike fishing. There are several types of depth finders, starting with a flasher and going all the way to color units that have mapping capabilities. Many come with a temperature gauge, and it is easy to see why that can be an important feature. (If your depth finder does not have this capability, there are inexpensive handheld units that will accurately gauge temperatures.) Both Vexilar and Minn-Kota offer these types of units. These will all work fine, as long as one can decipher the information they put out. A flasher, for instance, will tell you almost everything the other units will, but it is a bit more difficult to use and it takes longer to learn what it is telling you. I started with a flasher because that was all that was available at the time, and I still use one on some fly-in trips. But, given a choice, I'd go with one of the liquid-crystal graphs. They have come a long way since their inception, and can now tell you nearly everything and do it with fine detail.

The newest piece of electronic wizardry is the GPS (Global Positioning System) unit. These are very handy in many situations. For the guy setting out on an unfamiliar wilderness lake, these have opened up a whole new world. You can now go exploring anywhere without fear of getting lost. The GPS will show you the exact route you've taken, and will get you home in fine shape. You can mark spots of interest, or ones that have been productive, and return at a later date—even years later. They are also invaluable to the troller. If you happen upon a particularly productive pass, you can duplicate your path easily and makes runs over the exact same route. These units are, in my opinion, the best thing to happen to fishermen since the advent of the depth finder, and I consider them to be an essential tool in my boat. Many of the higher-end depth finders now incorporate GPS technology.

In addition, there are handheld GPS units available that do the job in fine fashion. I have a couple, with routes of several wilderness lakes marked on them, and I'm never out without one of them in the boat. There is one drawback, however. Because these are electronic units run by batteries, they will fail on occasion. For this reason, it is always best to have a lake map and a compass along and to keep an eye on where you are. Also, be sure to take an extra set of batteries along for those handheld units. Batteries can be changed without any loss of information stored in the unit.

Sunglasses

One last vital tool is polarized sunglasses—not only to protect your eyes from ultraviolet rays and flying hooks, but also for seeing into the water. If you have a big fish following, it is far better to know it before the fish reaches boatside, and all you see is its tail as it leaves. With polarized sunglasses, you can see the fish from a fair distance and attempt to make maneuvers that could cause it to strike. Additionally, these sunglasses can help to see hazardous conditions in the water before you run your motor into them. I am never on the water without them.

Leaders

Because of the pike's mouth full of incredibly sharp teeth, a bite-proof leader is an absolute necessity. Basically, there are two types of leaders: flexible and nonflexible leaders; both have specific uses. The flexible ones are used in most situations, and are the choice for all but gliding or stop-and-go-type lures. For those types of lures, you want a solid wire leader.

Flexible leaders are commonly made from several strands of light wire that may be uncoated, or coated with a plastic material. I use the coated kind. There is also the option of using fluorocarbon for a flexible leader. These types of leaders, because of their flexible nature, allow the lure more action, and I use these types at least 75 percent of the time. Most of the commercial leaders in a store will have connector sleeves to hold them together. I do not use these, and opt to make my own. (I'll explain how at the end of this segment. I use the same procedures to make my dead-bait rigs and wiring jigs.) The main reason I prefer to make my own leaders is that I do not trust connector sleeves. I have witnessed them fail, plus I can exert more quality control doing it myself and am able to pick the components to suit my needs. They are actually less expensive. I use expensive swivels on mine because I don't like leaving anything to chance, but these swivels are reusable and will last nearly forever. I also enjoy using something I made myself, and it is a great way to spend a bad winter day.

Solid wire leaders are the best choice for any stop-and-go or gliding-type lures, due to their intrinsic lack of action. The action is supplied by the angler's technique. Chuggers, gliding jerkbaits, and walk-the-dog-type lures all fall into this category.

After casting a gliding jerkbait out, the angler tightens his line, makes a sharp jerk, tightens the line, and jerks again. The lure will dive and glide to one side or the other. While this glide is a great strike-triggering maneuver, it is also where the trouble starts if a flexible leader is used. As the lure glides forward, that type of leader will, of course, flex. When it does, the gliding bait will catch up to it and the hooks become fouled in the leader. Now, with a solid wire leader, when the lure glides forward, it will push the leader out in front of it, keeping the leader completely away from the hooks.

I've heard a lot of talk about how great fluorocarbon leaders are, and how their invisibility adds up to so many fish. Perhaps I'm guilty of being from the old school, but I have never used fluorocarbon leaders. This is not to say I will never try fluorocarbon leaders—I like to keep an open mind in these matters and can envision certain situations where they could be advantageous, but I haven't made the switch yet. One possible advantage of using fluorocarbon that I can see is the fact that they are lighter in weight than wire, and this could help keep lighter-weight topwater baits from sinking.

And the invisibility factor? Well, I'm not too concerned with that. I've been chasing these critters for a long time and I do as well as most, and better than some. And I've been using the same leaders mentioned here for all of thirty years. They work for me, and they'll undoubtedly work for you, too.

Making Your Own

I started making my own leaders early in my pike-fishing career because I wasn't satisfied with commercially made ones. You can make these more inexpensively than you can buy them, and the quality is far better. I use the best-quality components I can find. The swivels may seem expensive at first, but they can be reused virtually forever. I do not reuse the snaps, however, as I believe that repeatedly opening and closing them will eventually weaken the wire.

Now let's look at how to make these leaders. I'll start with the flexible leaders.

The required components are:

1. Nylon-coated wire (I normally use 40-pound test)
2. Solid-ring ball-bearing swivels, #3
3. Cross-lock snaps, #6 or #9
4. Candle
5. Sharp knife
6. Wire cutter
7. Small vise-grip pliers or a hemostat

Components for making flexible leaders. ALL PHOTOS IN MAKING YOUR OWN SECTION BY MIKE TRETTIN

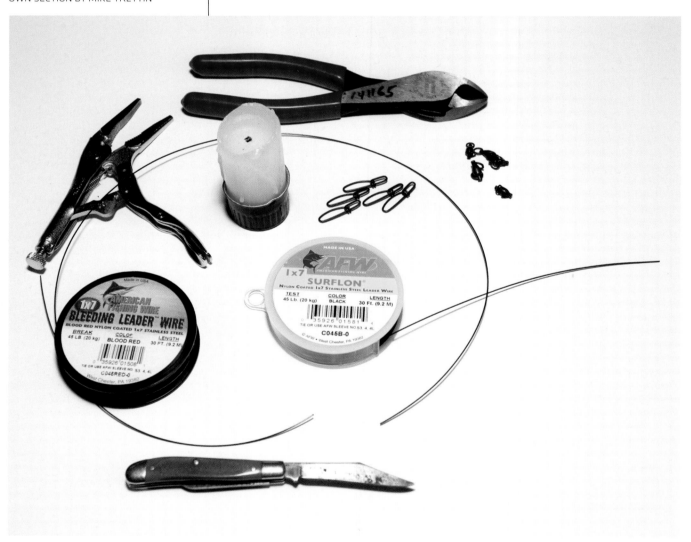

You must first decide how long a leader to use. For casting applications, I normally use one from 8 to 12 inches in length. For trolling, I like one about 24 inches long. Fish caught trolling tend to roll a lot, and the extra length will prevent line being cut by the fish's teeth or the sharp ridge on the gill flap.

So let's construct a 12-inch leader. You'll need a piece of coated wire about 18 to 20 inches long.

1. Thread the wire through the eye on the swivel (the end that turns), and clamp on the vise-grips about an inch up from the end of the wire. Gripping the swivel with one hand and the longer piece of wire in the other, allow 2 inches of wire, with the vise-grips attached, to hang from the swivel. Now, while still gripping the swivel and the main wire, twirl the vise-grip-held piece around the main wire, making at least five good wraps, or until the tag end is completely wrapped around the main wire and the grips are up against it.

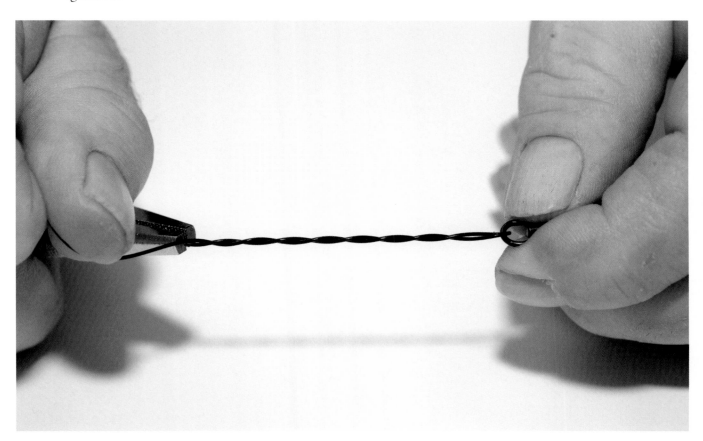

2. Using your thumb and forefinger to hold onto the grips and main wire, lower it to the lit candle and begin slowly passing it back and forth over the flame until it just starts to bubble and blister. At this point, you need to reduce the heat by raising the works up a little from the flame and making your passes quicker until the blistering disappears and the wraps take on a fluid, smooth look. If you are not quick enough in this maneuver, the coating on the wire will catch on fire, compromising the strength of the connection. If this happens, cut off the hardware and start over.

3. Remove from the flame, and blow on the wraps to cool them down. Then remove the vise-grips.

4. You should now have a piece of wire about 16 inches long, with a swivel on one end and a wrapped section that has a tag end about an inch long. You could take your wire cutters and try to cut that tag end off close to the last wrap, but you'll be leaving a sharp nub there that can leave a nasty scratch on your fingers, as well as gather weeds. A much better way is to take the knife, and starting as close to the wraps as possible, scrape away the coating from one side of the wire. Now, pry the remaining coating away from the wire and clip off the wire, keeping the coating intact.

5. Next, grip the wraps on one end and the main wire between your thumb and forefinger, using both hands. Lower this to the top of the flame and quickly roll it between those digits. You will see the tag end of coating shrink up around that sharp nub (we hope). Quickly remove from the flame, and before the coating cools completely, roll it between your thumb and forefinger to smooth it out and completely cover the nub. Do not be concerned if this leaves a bit of a bulge at the ends of the wraps; the pike don't seem to care, and the weeds will slide right off.

6. Do the same on the other end, but use a snap instead. You now have a completed leader of top-notch quality. The fused connection is strong enough to tow a car. The wire will break before that connection does, if it is constructed properly.

This may sound complicated, but it is easier than it sounds and much easier to do than to write a description about. Practice it a bit, and after a few times you will be making professional-grade leaders. I also use these same procedures for making bait rigs, wiring jigs, and hooks for soft plastics.

Making solid wire leaders is different, but no more difficult.

The tools required for this type of leader consist of:

1. Wire cutter
2. Single-strand wire
3. Haywire twist tool
4. Solid-ring ball-bearing swivels, #3
5. Cross-lock snap, #6 or #9

Some components for making solid wire leaders.

Haywire Twist tool.

I use what is known as a haywire twist on most of my single-strand leaders, and find it does the job well. One can make these leaders by hand without the use of the special tool mentioned, but you will find it far easier to accomplish with the tool, and suffer fewer holes poked in your fingers. Recently, I discovered such a tool that is much easier to use than the one I previously used. It is called a Haywire Twist Tool, and is made by the American Wire Company. This is one handy little device and is small enough that it could be carried in a tackle box and used in the field if needed. It is fairly easy to use and comes with good instructions. After a few attempts, you'll be making first-class leaders. Here is how it's done.

1. After cutting a length of wire, insert it through the armatures on the top of the tool. Feed the tag end of the wire through the swivel, and loop back around through the side hole.

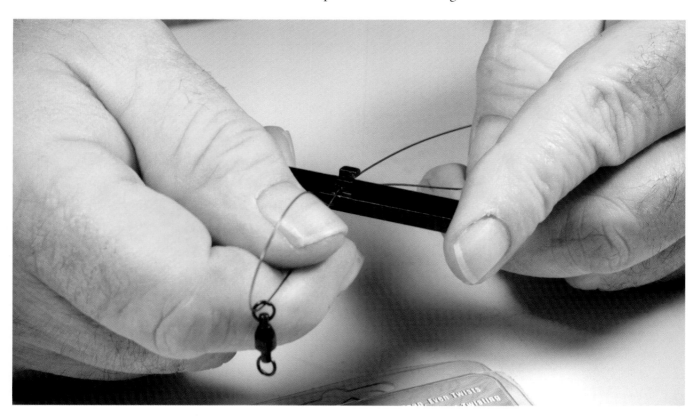

2. Pull the tag end through the opposite side hole until you have at least five inches protruding. While holding the loop and swivel stationary, twist the tool end-over-end in a clockwise direction approximately five times, while pulling the tool slightly away from the loop to form five long twists.

3. Slowly back the wires away from the tool while holding onto the loop until the tag end is free, and bend it to a 90-degree angle. Now remove the wire and put the tag end down through the hole on top and slide the main wire back under the armatures.

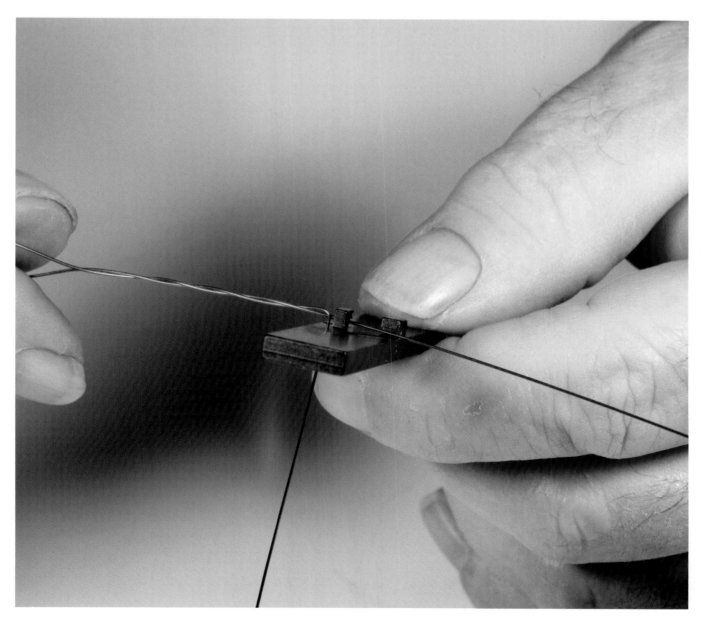

4. While holding the loop and swivel stationary, twist the tool end-over-end in a clockwise direction four or five turns while applying slight pressure towards the loop end to form the barrel wraps. Remove the leader from the tool. You should now have a connection of several loose wraps, ending with a section of tight barrel wraps, and a tag end protruding at least an inch.

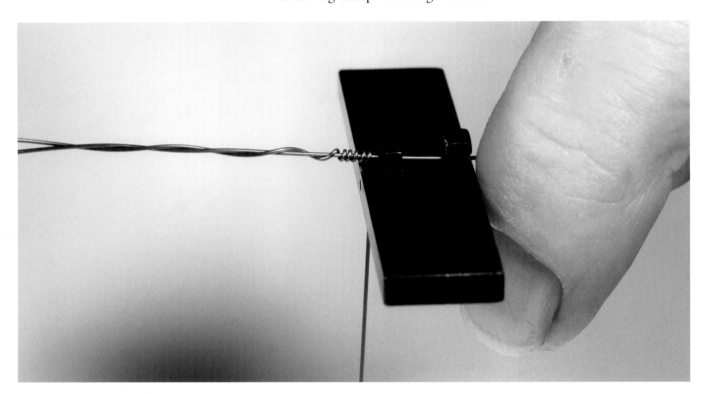

5. The next step, removing the tag end, is very important. You could use the wire cutters to cut it, but no matter how close to the wraps you cut it, there will still be a small nub remaining. This little nub can be downright dangerous, and I have scars on three fingers of my right hand to prove it. During the landing process for one fish, I grabbed hold of the leader to turn the big pike around when it made a mad dash and pulled the leader through my grip. That nub ripped through my fingers like a razor. The nub will also gather weeds like a garden rake. But there is a way to break that tag end off with no nub left behind. Simply bend the wire completely up 90 degrees and as close to the wraps as possible. Then bend it completely down in the same spot. By repeating this bending

several times, eventually the wire will break off in the middle of the barrel wraps, leaving no nub. If you do this correctly, you should be able to run the connection back and forth through your thumb and forefinger without feeling any snagging at all.

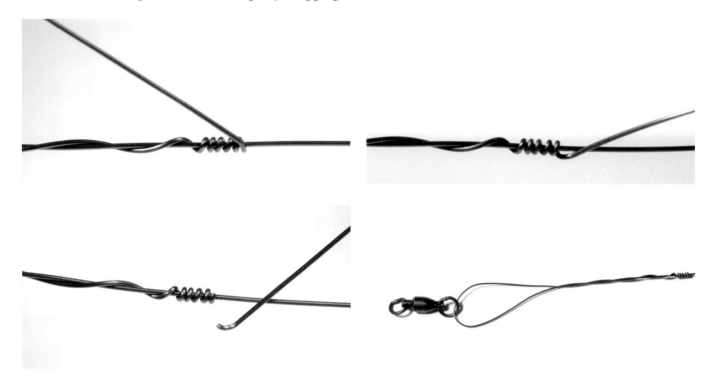

6. Repeat this process on the other end of the wire using a snap, and you will have a fine leader to use.

As I stated earlier, this can be also be done without the tool, using a pair of needle-nose pliers or a small vise-grips. But the tool is so much easier and quicker to use that I never make them by hand any more, and for that reason will not go into that discussion here. One other thing about using these single-strand leaders—once they develop a kink in the wire, change leaders. A slight bend in the wire is not going to weaken it, but a sharp bend or a kink will, and shouldn't be trusted.

CHAPTER FOUR

Ice-Out

Temperature range: 38 to 50 degrees

After so many months of frozen water, open water has finally arrived. This is a very special time for a pike fisherman, for this is the time when one's odds of catching that trophy of a lifetime are probably at their highest. You might ask, "What makes this period so special?"

The answer is simple: big fish are congregated in specific locations. Actually, chances are very good that the fisherman with the knowledge and the correct equipment, and who is on water that contains a healthy population of big pike, will catch multiple trophy pike in a single day.

Northern pike are the first freshwater fish to spawn. Many will complete their spawning under the ice pack. At the start of the open-water season, immediately after ice-out, pike will begin to prowl. Most have spawned by now and will begin to feed to recover from the rigors associated with the spawn. This feeding activity increases very gradually in intensity. Pike are programmed at this time to feed on dead fish. They slowly cruise the bottom, picking up dead fish that may have been trapped in a river or frozen in the ice. They provide pike with the caloric intake they need without requiring a lot of energy to obtain it.

Quick-Strike Rigs

All of the rigs that I use to present dead bait are of the quick-strike variety. In Europe, these types of rigs have been used for centuries. They were introduced to North America in the early 1980s through a joint effort by Jan Eggers of Holland and *In-Fisherman* magazine. The idea behind these rigs is to set the hook immediately when a pike picks up the bait, as opposed to the old method of waiting and letting the fish swallow it.

There are several advantages to using quick-strike rigs. First, and most importantly, when used correctly they are easy on the fish and make for successful releases. Also, the hookup ratio is very high—well over 90 percent. And they will usually be hooked in the corner of the mouth, making hook extraction simple and easy.

The Europeans have this bait fishing down to a science, with so many different rigs to cover their varying situations. I studied these for several

Some bait rigs, from top to bottom: bottom rig with non-sliding slip sinkers; floating-jig rig utilizing a floating frog lure; and bait suspended beneath a float with a rubber-core sinker.
MIKE TRETTIN

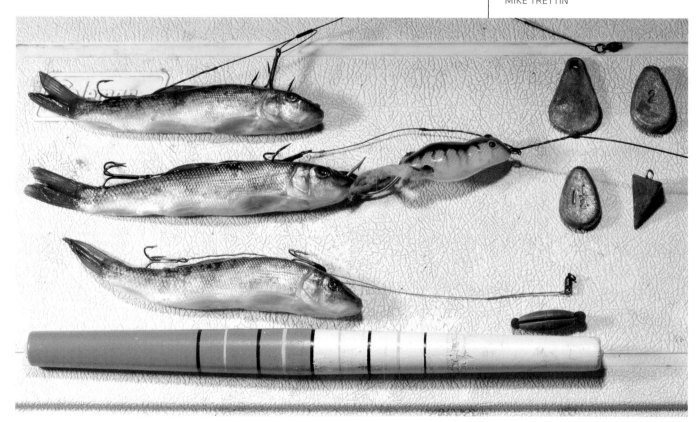

Author's note: The idea with these sinkers is to use those that allow the line to slip through the sinker (so the pike doesn't detect the sinker) while keeping it stationary on the bottom so that it is less likely to snag.

years and tried several of their techniques. However, I have reduced the number of rigs I use to just three, and find that these will cover all the situations I'm likely to face rather nicely. In Europe they fish bait rigs throughout their entire season, while I mostly just use them at ice-out.

It will be tough for the angler in North America to find a place to purchase these rigs, but you can easily make your own using the process I showed you earlier to fuse the coated wire together.

My dead-bait rigs, how to make them, and where and when to use them are as follows.

1. The basic bottom rig
2. The floating-jig rig
3. The bait-below-a-float rig

1. The Basic Bottom Rig

The basic bottom rig consists of a length of coated wire with two treble hooks and a sliding sinker. Large treble hooks are not needed to make these rigs successful. I normally use something like a number-two or -three Eagle Claw 374. The first treble hook down from the swivel is positioned on a loop held by an open connector, and the other treble is fixed to the end of the rig. This loop, along with the swinging treble, allows one to adjust the length of the rig to match the size of the bait. I'll take a bait and hold the rig up against it to see how long I need it, then add about an inch. Once I have the length determined, I simply pull on both ends and close the loop around the connector. This will hold the first treble firmly in place without slipping. Do not crimp this sleeve, as there is a chance you'll damage the wire. I place this treble just behind the head of the bait and then place the end treble near the tail, usually in the top. For a sinker, I use either a flat sinker or a pyramid sinker to prevent it from sliding along the bottom in areas of current flow, while allowing the line to pass freely through it. This rig can be used in just about any location, but I prefer it in areas of slow current or at the mouth of rivers.

2. The Floating-Jig Rig

I use the floating-jig rig in areas of increased current, such as in the wash-out hole below a waterfall. This will lift the bait up off the bottom a bit and make it easier for the pike to take. It is easy to construct, and is simply the bottom rig attached to a large floating-jig head. (In the photograph of this rig, I used a floating frog lure instead of the jig head.) The jig head also has the benefit of adding a color attractor to the rig. Oddly enough, this is sometimes necessary, and you may need to experiment with different colors to find the most productive one. I normally start with chartreuse, then try pink or white. As with most angling, it is best to let the pike tell you their preferences on a particular day. I use the same non-sliding slip sinkers with this rig.

3. The Bait-below-a-Float Rig

Fishing bait below a float is actually not that much different, but you use a large float to both suspend the bait and act as a strike indicator. Here, I use a different sinker. Most times I use the same rig as when fishing on the bottom, but I use a rubber-core sinker attached to the line above the rig. For floats, the best one I've found is made by Float-Hi Float Company in Alexandria, Kentucky. They come in both weighted and unweighted models.

I always use an 11-inch-long unweighted model. With the weighted models, the float stands straight up. In wind or current, the float will lean and bob, and it is hard to distinguish a light bite. The unweighted model lies flat on the surface, and the 11-inch model will do it even with a fairly large bait and a sinker of ⅜ to ½ ounce. With this model, when a pike even just mouths the bait, the float will tilt, alerting the angler immediately. The weighted one will just go down an inch or so and is very hard to detect.

I prefer to use these rigs in areas with limited current flow, like slack-water areas near an incoming river or creek. Try to place the bait in the main channel, as this serves as their travel route. I also use these in washout holes and let the bait drift so it comes to rest on the side of the hole.

Bait

The type of bait to use is yet another matter to consider. The very best bait will be something that lives in the water being fished. That doesn't mean, however, that nothing else will work. I prefer to use soft-finned species, like suckers, ciscoes, or river chubs. Those three species represent my favorite choices, in that order. All are oily, soft-finned species. Pike will eat almost anything they can grab, but at this time of year, due to their scavenging nature, they are looking for something dead. These species represent baitfish that often suffer winterkill, and occur in most lakes where pike reside.

Consider a case in which you are heading out on the water with two dozen frozen suckers. You pull up, anchor in a hole below a rapids area, cast out a nice sucker rigged up on a float rig, and immediately get a bite. After landing the fish and releasing the pike, you reach for another sucker and cast it out. It doesn't take even a minute and you've got another bite. So, naturally you set the hook, fight the fish and land it, then release it too. At that rate, in less than an hour you are going to run out of bait. If you are in a good spot, this is a very likely scenario.

To conserve on bait, I use rubber bands. By wrapping the bait with a rubber band just behind its head, you'll save bait without affecting the hookup ratio. Keeping the band as far away from the rear treble as possible allows that rear hook enough room to break free and travel a few inches before coming into contact with the band. This is plenty of room to complete the hookup, and you can now use that same bait again. Even

Some modified rigs that can be used in Ontario and other locations with comparable regulations. Note the four hook-points on each rig. MIKE TRETTIN

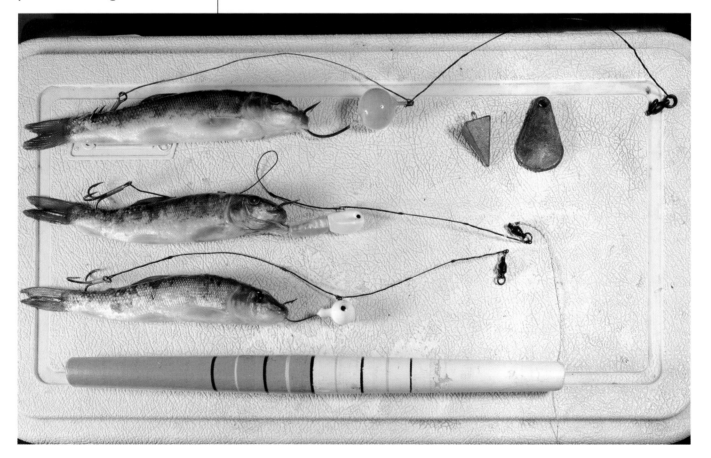

when you're on a hot bite, you can use that same bait until it will barely hold a hook. Those big pike don't care if it is shredded. If it is dead and smells like something they'd eat naturally, it will get attacked.

Considerations When Using Quick-Strike Rigs

There are a couple of very important aspects to fishing quick-strike rigs. The first is their proper use. As the name implies, you strike quickly with these rigs instead of the traditional method of letting the fish run with the bait and swallowing it. With both bottom-fishing rigs, cast them out and let them get to the bottom. Then tighten your line and take out all of the slack. Once the line is tight, lower the rod tip, and, keeping it close to water level, pull off about a foot of line from the reel. Using this approach, sit with the rod in one hand while holding the foot of slack line in the other. When a pike picks up the bait, you will feel it as pressure on the slack line. When the pike pulls the slack line tight, set the hook as hard as possible. Do not let the fish run beyond the length of that slack foot of line.

With the float rig, set the hook as soon as that big bobber tilts. I'm constantly amazed at the hookup ratio when using these rigs; I miss very few fish.

The second consideration in using these types of rigs is their legality. For reasons unknown to me, there are places where they are outlawed. Ontario is one such place, where you can only have four points on a bait rig. However, there are a few modifications you can make to render the rigs completely legal. For the bottom rigs, I use a regular jig head with a treble-hook stinger and a sliding sinker. And the floating-jig head can be rigged with just the rear treble instead of two trebles; it is still nearly as effective, and is now considered a floating jig with a stinger hook. It is almost the same for fishing bait below a float. Instead of using the rig mentioned, make your rigs with a ⅜-ounce jig with a rear treble stinger. The jig acts as the sinker. Hookup ratios are also very high using these methods. It is always best to check local regulations before heading out.

The last consideration in using these techniques is one of responsibility. This is a very effective method of targeting the biggest pike in a given system. If the proper techniques are not used, it is very easy to damage the ecosystem by removing or killing the large predators. Big pike are probably at their most vulnerable position during the ice-out period—catches of multiple huge pike are not only possible, but often probable. It is critical to the future of the fishery to practice effective (and proper) catch and release.

Locations in Lakes

Water temperatures for this technique will range from 38 degrees to almost 50 degrees. In lakes, pike will spawn in the back of dark-bottomed bays. The best bays will feature some sort of incoming water, perhaps a small creek or river. The big females swim through vegetation, randomly depositing their eggs, which adhere to the reeds and weeds. It is here that one should begin

Following a creek to a pothole.
JACK PENNY

the search. (A map is very helpful when exploring the best bays.) One nice thing about these techniques is that they are easily applied by the shore-bound angler. No boat is needed, as long as he can access these areas.

Check the map and look for bays with creeks flowing into them. Follow one of these creeks up, and if you encounter a pothole, you may have discovered a bonanza. Pike utilize these potholes as nurseries, and will use the creek as their highway to travel into and out of the area. If there is enough water in the creek, follow it to the pothole and try dead baits at the mouth and next to the shoreline weeds. Not all of these potholes will pay off, but enough will to make them worth checking out. Another hotspot is where the creek flows into the main bay. Pike will cruise the creek to and from the pothole, and setting up at the opening could score handsomely. Try to place your bait in the creek channel.

Another spot where a river enters a lake. Notice the float close to shore, sitting in the main channel. JACK PENNY

Locations in Rivers

In rivers, I look for holes with current. Waterfalls are a prime example. That rushing water scours out a large hole beneath the falls, and dead fish coming down the river will settle down on the bottom. A good strategy is to anchor off to the side of the hole and try to place your bait either right on the rim or on the sloping side just below the rim. The float rig works very well here. You can cast out and let it drift until the bait rests against the side. If you decide to try one of the bottom rigs, make sure you are using a sinker that will not roll or slide on the bottom. If your sinker slides on that sloping side, you'll end up with a sinker wedged in between rocks or in a crevice. The floating jig works very well right up on the rim of the hole.

A similar spot is below rapids. Pike may be found in slack-water areas off to the side of and downstream from the rapids to the first significant dropoff. The bottom rig works well here, as does the floating-jig head, and in the slack water they sometimes prefer it suspended below the float. Another place to check is a hole or trough on an outside bend in the river. Anchor upstream and try to place your bait on the upstream edge. The current will carry the scent of your bait into the hole and pike will follow that scent trail to the bait.

CHAPTER FIVE

Spring

Temperature range: 45 to 60 degrees

When water temperatures reach about 45 to 50 degrees, the metabolism of those big female pike will start to increase. Yes, they can still be taken on dead bait, but for those who would prefer to cast to them, this marks the start of the season.

Locations in Lakes

In lakes, those same spawning bays still hold the now-spawned-out females as well as the smaller males. While planning your strategies, there are several effective options to consider. First, the most productive bays will have wind blowing into them. In fact, this is an important key throughout the open-water season. At this time in the bays, swarms of minnows head into newly growing vegetation in anticipation of their spawn, and pike take full advantage of this situation. It is fairly common to hear the commotion as the pike go on the attack. If you are in a bay and hear a lot of splashing, follow it—it is the sound of opportunity. And that opportunity is to engage

The author's daughter Janelle with guide Darren Benellick. She caught this 46-inch pike in 2 feet of water on a small topwater lure. JACK PENNY

in what I consider the most enjoyable technique of all: topwater lures. And without question, this is the very best topwater bite of the entire season.

Smaller bass-sized lures work best here. The ideal lure will be one that can be retrieved slowly while remaining on top. I like to keep several different styles with me, and I let the pike dictate which is best. One day they might prefer something like a Nip-A-Diddee, with propellers on both ends.

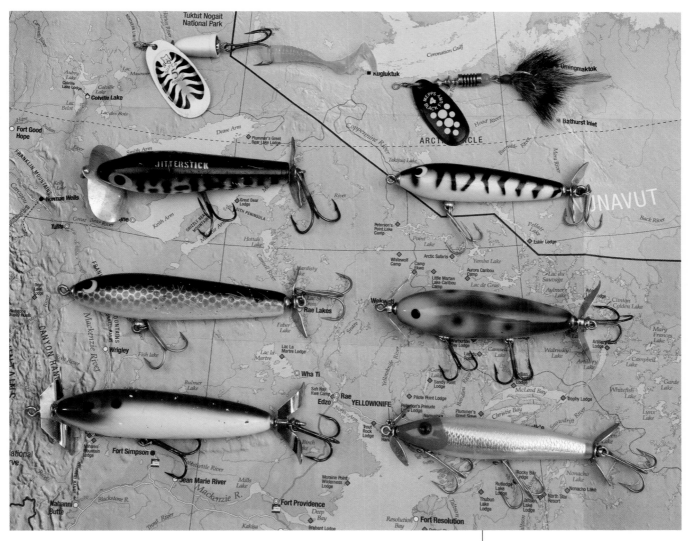

The next day it might be something a bit quieter like a Zara Spook. The buzzbaits that bass fishermen use will also draw a lot of strikes some days, but because they require a quicker retrieve to stay on top, they don't hook as many as a lure that can be worked more slowly. As always, the pike will tell you what they prefer, and it can change from day to day. It is best to carry a few different styles of topwater baits to give them a choice.

Another good lure in these bays is an inline spinner, like a number-3 or -4 Mepps or Blue Fox spinner. These can also be retrieved at a fairly slow pace and are exceptionally good hookers. I especially like to throw these in areas of newly grown sparse reeds. Spinners with a dressed hook always seem more productive to me, and I usually start with one featuring a white hair trailer. A great addition for plain inline spinners is a small strip of sucker belly meat or a walleye gullet, but be sure to check local regulations

Larger topwater lures work well on sand flats, as well as the jig.
MIKE TRETTIN

as this is not legal everywhere. A small twister-tail impaled on one point of the treble will work well too.

Other locations where topwater lures excel at this time are sand flats and beaches, where suckers and crawfish are plentiful. Pike roam these flats and beaches searching for them. A larger lure can be used here. If possible, I like to drift across these flats and beaches, casting randomly. In clear-water environments, I'll try to get a position high up in the boat so I can better see down into the water. Of course, polarized sunglasses are essential for this. At times, you can spot pike cruising, and if the topwater lure doesn't trigger them, I cast a large jig in front of them. Most times, that will seal the deal. A black jig with about a 6-inch grub or a comparably sized Reaper has proven very effective on the sand. Under the right conditions, a soft plastic crawdad crawled along the bottom will also get bitten by any pike that sees it.

In the backs of the bays where a creek is flowing in, you will see yellowed dead reeds left over from the previous year. Some will be broken or bent over, forming a tangled jungle. If you find a spot like this that has wind blowing into it, pike will most likely be in there. But it can be difficult to fish because of the tangled mess. A weedless presentation is needed, and treble hooks are out of the question here. Weedless spoons and plastics, though, will do the job. Cast a Johnson Silver Minnow back in there and drag it across the top while letting it fall into open pockets. Or use a weedless plastic lure; something like a Slug-Go or a frog works well. Pause them in open pockets, and either let them float or slowly sink . . . and be ready. One word of caution is needed here—use heavy equipment, as the pike will surely dive into that mess when it is hooked.

Crankbaits are another viable option in spring. Try a shallow-diving crankbait around the mouth of incoming creeks. Suckers will run in these creeks during this period, and jerking a shallow crank will sometimes produce explosive strikes. Choose a dark-backed lure to simulate those

suckers. Sometimes a slow, straight retrieve works best, but don't discount jerking it across the surface. Suspending crankbaits are also great lures at this time. My favorite is the Rapala Husky Jerk in sizes 8, 10, and 12. I prefer to bring them in with a jerk-and-pause retrieve. I find a good cadence to be jerk, jerk, jerk, pause. Once you see a pike take an interest, pause the lure and just let it sit there hovering. Pike will lie there transfixed by the lure, sometimes for quite a while, before smashing into it. Actually, it is great fun watching them and seeing how long they can take it before coming unglued. At this time of year, a very high percentage will eventually hit it if you can wait them out. I've watched pike stare at that lure for several minutes before finally charging it.

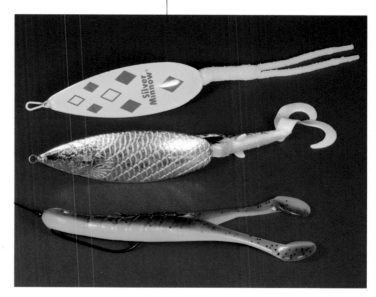

Crankbaits come in two basic materials, hard plastic and wood. With wooden lures, you run the risk of not getting the hooks into the fish, because a pike's teeth are so sharp that at times they will embed in the bait, and it won't slide in their mouths to allow proper hook sets.

The mouth of an incoming creek. Suckers will run in locations like this, and big pike will follow them. JACK PENNY

The same applies to jointed crankbaits. The teeth tend to catch in the joint, preventing a good hookup. With hard plastic, the lure slides nicely through the mouth and you'll be able to achieve a much better hookup ratio. This is not to say that wooden or jointed lures have no use, but be aware of their limitations.

The next spring lure option in lakes is the jig. I like casting a lighter-weight jig dressed with either a black twister tail or a dark strip of bunny hair. When retrieved with a slow lift-and-drop retrieve, these resemble leeches and can be the hottest lure in your box. Another productive jig is one that a lot of bass fishermen employ. Skirted jigs that they use for flipping a jig-and-pig are perfect. Look for one in a dark color with the eye coming out the pointed nose of the jig. I usually tip these with a black twister tail, and use them if I spot a big fish lying in the sparse reeds that has ignored my other offerings. If all else fails on this fish, here's a little trick to try. First, cast the jig well past the pike and retrieve it just fast enough to keep it off the bottom. Try to bring it past the fish about five feet in front of her with a slow lift-and-lower maneuver.

If the pike still doesn't take it, make another cast and try to bring it down the same path, but stop it in front of the fish about five feet out and let it sit for several seconds. Now give it a small hop, and let it sit still again. If she hasn't moved on it in a few seconds, give it one more hop and stop. If after several seconds she still hasn't moved toward it, just let it sit there. The silicon skirt on the jig will be moving around and looking alive, and this is often enough to unnerve the pike into pouncing on it. If not, start to shake your rod, keeping the jig stationary. This maneuver will add vibration and make the jig appear to struggle. At times, pike will make a mad rush and attack the jig. Other times they may just move slowly up, turn slightly on their side, and suck it in. Not all pike will fall for this trick, but some will. It is far better than just giving up, boating on, and wondering what you could have done.

This warrants another word of caution about stalking these pike in shallow water. Silence is golden. Fish have a vibration-detecting sensory system, called a lateral line, running along their sides. Because of their length, big pike naturally have a longer lateral line, which equates to more sensitive "hearing" and are therefore more prone to spook. Because of this, silence is imperative for success. Oddly enough, pike don't seem bothered by the low drone of an outboard motor, but any sharp noises like something dropped in the boat or a jig banged against the side of the boat will greatly diminish your chances.

In recent years, I have seen some writers refer to spoons as somewhat "has been" lures, and suggest that they are no longer effective. In my experience, nothing is further from the truth. If used correctly, spoons produce all year long and in nearly any situation, with the exception of the dead-bait period.

One problem I believe many anglers have is improper retrieval speed. Let me use two of my favorite spoons, the Dardevle and the Johnson Silver Minnow, to illustrate my point. The Dardevle was invented and released to the public in 1906, and the Silver Minnow came out in 1930. Now think about the equipment that fishermen had available back then. Reels, which control retrieval speed, were not made with 5-to-1 gear ratios, but were instead much slower, like 2 to 1. These spoons were designed to be used with much slower reels than are available today, so it is easy to see that the modern angler needs to slow down when using spoons. The ideal action of a spoon is a slow, back and forth rocking wobble. To achieve this, we use the slowest-ratio reels we can find, and still have to crank them slowly. If you notice that the spoon completely rotates or spins, it is being overpowered and you need to reduce the speed. Additionally, we always use some sort of trailer on them, and I will cover this more later on in the book.

Spoons will be productive in nearly all locations at one time or another. In early spring, I find it best to use smaller spoons and increase the size as the season moves on. I'm often asked which color is best, and there is no way to specify a single color. A good rule (which the old-timers used to tell me) is silver on a sunny day and gold or copper on a cloudy day. This is a good place to start, but there's more to be considered than just that. (Keep in mind that these suggestions apply to all lures.) Water clarity and color are good examples. What works well in very clear water may not be the best choice for a tannin-stained lake. And murky water is something else again. Additionally, pike sometimes exhibit local preferences. What seems to work well in one lake may not be the best choice in a lake twenty miles down the road, even though the water is comparable in color. As it always is, experimentation is an important key to success.

Spoon colors and pattern choices for clear water. MIKE TRETTIN

In waters containing a lake trout population, the water is clear, and being able to see the bottom clearly at forty feet presents both advantages and challenges. For one thing, you can spot pike a long way off. On the other side of that coin, however, they can see you just as clearly, so long casts are usually mandatory. Plus, pike in these waters seem to prefer something that looks natural. For this reason, I try to use natural colors and patterns. Browns, black and white, red and white, and greens are all good choices. My best patterns include perch, pike, walleye, sucker, and the like. Pike living in this kind of water are able to get a much better look at a lure, so one that appears as lifelike as possible is most likely to get the desired results. Shown here are some of my picks for fishing in clear water. Some of the spoons have been repainted to get the desired patterns and colors.

Tannin-stained water is usually still clear, but appears dark colored, like tea. This is caused by decaying vegetation, and is probably the most common type of water in pike country. I still use some of the same offerings as I do in clear water, but find that louder colors have their place here as well. Yellow, gold, chartreuse, red, green, and metallic colors are good examples. And patterns don't need to be nearly as precise as in clear water.

Some color choices for tannin-stained water. MIKE TRETTIN

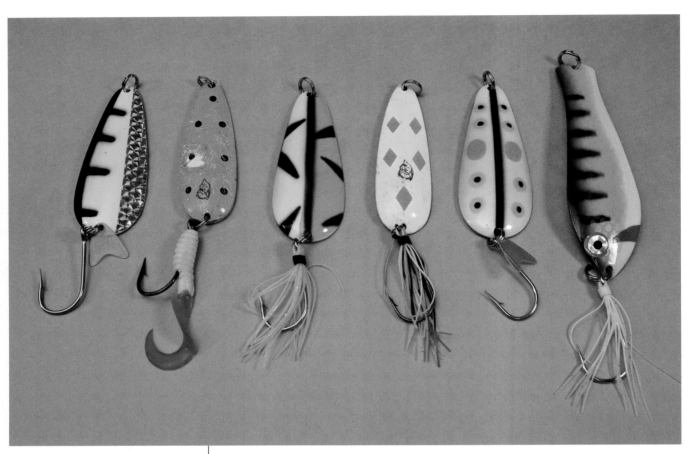

Spoon choices for murky water.
MIKE TRETTIN

Muddy or murky water can present different challenges to the piker. As you would imagine, pike can't see nearly as well in this type of water. For this reason, the lateral line becomes more significant in their search for food. I always use loud colors here, but also incorporate more vibration in my lure choices. With spoons, this means one that gives off more thump and wobble. Spinnerbaits will have bigger blades, and crankbaits will have rattles. This will help the pike to home in on the lure more easily.

During the latter part of this period, when water temperatures reach somewhere around 50 degrees, pike can be found around rocks, especially in the warm afternoons. Pike typically will feed heavily and seek the warmth of shallow rocks to rest and digest. These fish will often be inactive and refuse most offerings. We discovered a little trick to deal with these stubborn pike, quite by accident. Mary and I drifted into a rocky creek mouth, and while standing on the front deck, I saw numerous huge pike lying on the bottom in less than three feet of water. But we couldn't get any of them to bite. It wasn't until we had drifted over them and spooked several that Mary cast toward those spooked fish with a topwater lure. It

Shallow water with outcropping of rocks. JACK PENNY

was nabbed on the first cast. We just needed to get the pike stirred up and they would hit. We caught several big ones that afternoon on slow-moving topwater baits. What a gas.

Locations in Rivers

River fishing at this time offers its own opportunities. Early on, look for a hole or trough, anchor, and lower a ¼- to ⅜-ounce jig tipped with a 3-inch twister tail grub to the bottom. If you start catching walleyes, you can be sure you are in the right spot. Lower that jig to the bottom, raise it up two to four inches, and let it sit motionless. Do not jig it up and down; you'll get too many walleyes that way, and pike will ignore it for the most part. By letting it sit motionless, you will still catch plenty of walleyes, but every so often a big pike will slowly cruise through, and if it comes upon the jig, it will gobble it up. If you are catching walleyes one after another and they quit all of a sudden, this is a good sign that a big pike is in the area, so get ready.

Author's wife, Mary, with a nice northern caught on a swimbait in slack water, off the side of heavy current. JACK PENNY

Another productive location in rivers is the slack water beside areas of moderate-to-heavy current, such as waterfalls or rapids. Pike are ambush predators, and these slack-water areas are perfect spots for them to lie in wait for their next victim. This technique produces best later in the spring and on into early summer. Nearly all the aforementioned lures will work in this spot, but one that shines is the swimbait. There are two types that I use. One has an internal lead head with a soft plastic body formed around it, and the other looks like a crankbait with a diving bill and a soft, segmented plastic body.

My favorite strategy in this area is to anchor off the current in the upstream portion of the eddy, cast out into the current, and allow the lure to be swept downstream until it reaches the lower end of the slack water. Closing the reel bail will cause the bait to be swept into the slack water, and then I begin my retrieve back upstream through the eddy.

A swimbait with the internal jig head inside can either be jigged off the bottom or given a straight retrieve. The other style (without the internal jig head) is made to be swum, but I find that by changing the rod angles during the retrieve, I get significantly more hits. If you watch baitfish, they do not swim in a straight line for long. Instead, they will go a few feet in one direction, and then change and go a few feet in a different direction. By changing the position of your rod back and forth, you are mimicking this action. As always, of course, it is best to let the pike tell you which will be the best retrieve on a given day.

Some examples of preferred swimbaits for pike. MIKE TRETTIN

Dams and Dens

One prime location in both rivers and lakes are structures built by beavers, particularly dams and dens. The upstream side of a dam normally features a pool of water that is deeper than the river, and holds several meal choices for the hungry pike. Suckers, chubs, and walleyes all use these holes because beavers are vegetarians and won't bother them. Beaver dens, those piles of sticks and logs you occasionally see on the banks, are also fish magnets, especially in the spring. Look for dens on the north shorelines. Those sticks and logs warm up from the sun and kick the food chain into motion. Minnows congregate there, drawing in perch and walleyes to feed on them. Pike won't be far behind in either of these spots.

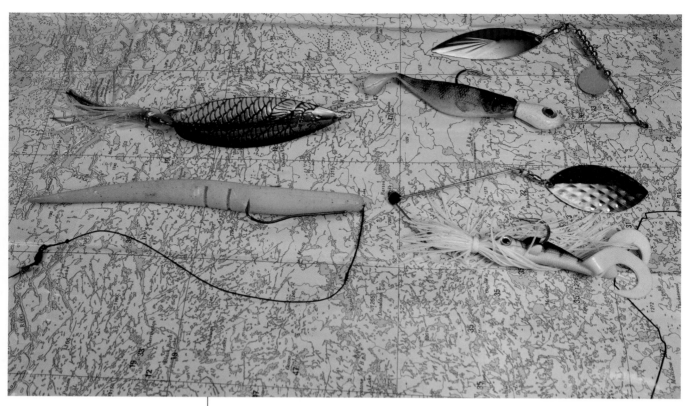

Good baits to try around structures in beaver habitat.
MIKE TRETTIN

There are a lot of snags around these beaver structures, and many are submerged and can't be seen. For this reason, I use weedless presentations here. Weedless spoons and spinnerbaits are great starting lures if the pike seem aggressive. If not, try soft plastic jerkbaits like a Slug-Go or any weedless plastics.

CHAPTER SIX

Summer

Temperature range: 55 degrees and above

Locations in Lakes: Bays

As the water temperature continues to climb into the mid-50-degree range, pike begin to move out of the shallows. The first place to check is the middle of the bay where the water gets a bit deeper. As always, look in bays that have wind blowing into them. The weed growth has risen by now and offers the pike plenty of places to hide and feed. Their metabolism has risen also, and they are now more willing to chase something down. This increased activity level bodes well for the pike fisherman. I prefer to start with an aggressive presentation here. Faster retrieves and more erratic action on the lures work well on most days.

On the odd off-days, I will try a more subdued presentation, like a soft plastic jerkbait or a jig-and-lizard, but those days are few at this time of year. Start your search at the first significant dropoff. Fan-cast the areas on both sides of the boat, but try to keep your lure in the upper half of the water column, above most of the emerging cabbage. These pike will be active and looking for something swimming by, instead of scrounging off the bottom. I like to start casting straight off the side of the boat and work my way around the boat until I'm casting straight out the other side. After making a couple of passes in this manner, I'll switch lures and start again if nothing has struck. A good example would be to start on the left side of the boat and cast to the 9 o'clock position with a 1-ounce Dardevle. The next cast will be at about the 9:30 position. Then 10 o'clock. Make your way around the boat until you hit the 3 o'clock position and reverse direction, casting all the way back to the 9 o'clock position. You are now covering most of the area around you.

After making a couple of trips around the clock, change to a spinnerbait if nothing has happened. If you are doing this while anchored, change positions after covering the area with several different lures. If you are drifting, try to make different passes so you cover as much of the area as possible. Be persistent in your search. Don't get in a hurry and move out too quickly. By doing so you might just miss the pike of a lifetime. I have had experiences where we drifted over the same spot for a couple of hours, catching many small-to-medium pike, and all of a sudden, from out of nowhere, here comes grandma pike and she snatches the lure. Persistence does pay off.

Points

After covering the bay, check the points at its entrance. This will be the next stop on a pike's migration to cooler climes, and it is a good spot for heavier spoons. A slimmer-bodied spoon, like an Eppinger Cop-E-Cat, is made to be retrieved quicker. I like the 2-ounce size because I can cast it a long way and it has great action. Again, a faster, more erratic retrieve will likely do the trick but experimentation is usually necessary. Gibbs Tackle has a spoon named Kit-A-Mat that has been very effective in these spots. It is a small peanut-shaped spoon that is thick, so it is heavy for its size. Cabela's carries a similar spoon in their Real Image line as well. These are both great spoons in several situations, and excel on these points.

These points can also be trolled. Pike will be found in middepths at this time of year and start to move to rocks. Some spoons troll well, but crankbaits are my favorite here. We've taken giant pike trolling minnow-type crankbaits over rocky points and adjacent shorelines in early summer. Shad Raps, especially the Super Shad Rap, are very productive also. I

Top to bottom: Cop-E-Cat, Real Image, Kit-A-Mat. MARY PENNY

troll these areas by weaving in and out in a narrow "S" pattern, covering different depths. The line doesn't need to be extremely far back; a good long cast will do fine. By keeping an eye on your electronics, you will see pods of baitfish hanging around these spots and pike will be there to feed on them. If you see these pods, work this area extensively.

By the time temperatures reach about 65 degrees, nearly all of the big pike will be in search of cooler temperatures. This is a time when a lot of fishermen see their success rates take a nosedive and have a tough time catching the bigger fish. The smaller pike are still in the shallows and easy to catch, and the excuse I've heard most often for the lack of big fish goes something like, "The bigger pike shed their teeth and get sore gums, so they won't bite." This is not the case. Everything has to eat to survive, and pike do not gum their food. As temperatures rise, so does the metabolism of the pike, and they must feed more often. And naturally, when they feed more, there is a greater chance they will lose teeth. This presents no

Super Shad Raps for trolling rocky points. MIKE TRETTIN

problems, though; pike will replace their teeth quickly. No, the deal is that the big pike have moved, and to catch them we have to move, too.

Weeds

Okay; they move, but to where? In lakes, some of them will move to main lake open-water areas to feed on roving schools of some species, like ciscoes and whitefish. Others will find comfort in the shade of weeds. Let's look at those weed fish first. One kind of weed that draws pike during warmer periods is the water lily. Lily pads that grow in current areas are the best ones now. They provide shade, and the current tends to run cooler. A weedless presentation is best here—the stalks on those lilies are tough, and if you hook one with a treble it is difficult to pull free. A weedless spoon with a trailer is a good bet in this location. Most of the soft plastics that are

Lily pads in current areas provide shade and are good areas to probe with weedless lures.
JACK PENNY

weedless will work well too. A Slug-Go, slowly sinking and darting around among the stalks, will unglue a lot of pike, and a topwater frog, jerked across the pads and paused in between, can also bring explosive strikes.

There is another important weed of which you should be aware. Scientists call it *Potamogeton amplifolius*. Some people may refer to it as the largeleaf pondweed, but most of the rest of us just call it cabbage. No matter what you call it, cabbage represents the best of the best in weeds. Cabbage will have broad, pointed leaves that are attached to a slender stem. Look for cabbage that is nice and green with no slime or scum on it. The best cabbage beds will also have deep water somewhere nearby. Just how deep is relative to the lake you're on. Some lakes may have an average depth of fifteen feet and may bottom out at twenty-five; others could be three times that. Look for weed beds that start shallow and gradually run deeper. The longer the incline, the better a weed bed it is. Once you've found that, the last key element is wind or water movement. It doesn't necessarily have to be current; wave action will suffice. But water movement is imperative, as a good chop on the water seems to rile up those big females.

As you make your approach, look for the edge where the tops of the cabbage just start to emerge. The submerged weeds create a feeding shelf and indicate the start of your search; then gradually work deeper. A weedless spoon is a great choice here, too. Tipping one with a single or twin-tailed grub is a good idea. Mary likes using a squid-shaped trailer, often used by salmon fishermen, and it is very effective. I find that weedless spoons are far more productive with a trailer.

Another good option here is the spinnerbait. Grinding a spinnerbait through cabbage can pay off in a very big way. Cast the spinnerbait out into the cabbage and let it sink. Then point your rod tip directly at the lure and begin cranking it in. It is important to keep that rod tip pointed at the bait. As you are cranking on the reel, you will feel the spinnerbait bumping and sliding through the weeds. If it hangs up, just keep cranking. Do not move the rod.

If it is hung up badly and won't come out, just pull the rod straight back, keeping the tip pointed at the lure. The spinnerbait will travel in a straight up-and-down orientation, and will make its way through the weeds as long as the rod tip is pointed at it. If you jerk the rod up or sideways, the spinnerbait will turn on its side and become hopelessly tangled. If you pull straight back, it will eventually come through.

With spinnerbaits, I prefer a Colorado blade for working the mid-depths and a willow-leaf blade for deeper-water weeds. Another productive bladed bait is an inline spinner like a Mepps. These work best when retrieved just over the tops of submerged cabbage. My preference here is one that is larger than those used in the spring. I've had great success using a Mepps Muskie Magnum in both white and fire-tiger. A number-5 Blue Fox Vibrax is another good one. I like to impale a one-inch Power Grub on one tine of the treble of the plain models.

There is another way to approach the weed-bed fish, using wind to cover areas. Drifting with a jig-and-lizard is one of the easiest and most effective techniques to use. Study the wave patterns and see how they go across the cabbage. Then motor up, pick out a lane, and turn the boat sideways, leaving the motor running in neutral so position adjustments can be made easily. Cast out upwind, keeping the line short enough so the lizard is easily visible. You can now drift along, lifting the lizard up

A variety of spinnerbaits and inline spinners for working cabbage beds. MIKE TRETTIN

over weeds and letting it fall back into open pockets. This can get pretty exciting too, as you'll be able to see many of the strikes.

When using jigs, connect your leader directly to the jig instead of using a snap. They are a lot more weedless this way. Also, look for a jig with the eye coming straight out the front of a pointed nose. I like to use the Esox Cobra jigs and I also like the pyramid and swimming jigs that Thorne Brothers in Minneapolis sells. But almost any jig with a strong hook, and the eye coming out a pointed nose, will work—it will come through the weeds much better with this eye placement.

You can also try using unweighted dive-and-rise jerkbaits, like the Suick, the Burt, and the Squirrely Burt. You can use these lures drifting across the submerged weeds, giving them short jerks to keep them from diving too deeply. You can also troll these lures by going very slowly and giving the lure the same short jerk. It is best

Lizards can be a good choice for drifting cabbage beds. Note that the leaders are tied directly to the jigs. MIKE TRETTIN

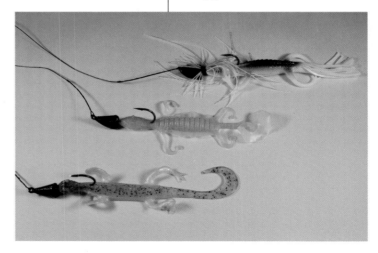

to use stout tackle when fishing these in thick cabbage beds. When these pike bite, they normally do so with vigor and will immediately dive into the jungle.

Open Water

Fishing the Rocks

The big pike that migrate to open water require a different approach, and the next patterns for summer pike will all involve rocks. We're looking for wind blowing into rocks. Look for rocky points, reefs, submerged boulders, or just a rocky shoreline. Any time the wind is blowing into them, these spots are all worth checking out. If you find a spot where the waves crashing into rock have created a mud line, concentrate considerable effort there. The food chain is in high gear here, and pike will be actively feeding.

A word of caution: Because of heavy wave action, it is often best for safety's sake if only one angler is casting while the other one runs the motor to keep from crashing into the rocks. Big fish are found here, and there is

Windblown rocks like these are pike magnets. JACK PENNY

just no way to safely operate the boat and fight one of these big pike. If you catch a big pike in this spot, you can bet it is not alone. This is a prime feeding spot under these conditions, and big pike will congregate here. There are normally enough so that one angler can catch a couple, then motor out to deeper water and switch positions with his partner and let him catch a couple.

This pattern is a run-and-gun affair. Not every wind-blown rocky shoreline or point is going to hold a pack of hungry water wolves. Pull up and make fifteen to twenty casts: If they're there, you'll know it. If not, move on and look for another wind-blown spot, or just move down the same shoreline to another position. The feeding binges the pike have in these spots do not last all day, so it is best to check them several times. However, if you do catch one here, don't be too quick to move if you don't hook up again right away. There may just be a lull in their feeding activity, and by catching one you may excite the others into another frenzy.

Bait choices vary. All those lures used in the weeds will work here as well, but my first choice is a crankbait, especially one I can cast a long way. Bomber Magnum Long A's have served us well for years in these spots.

Top to bottom, starting at the left: a couple of Bomber Magnum Long A's, two jointed Stalkers, two Super Stalkers, and two Squirrely Jakes. MIKE TRETTIN

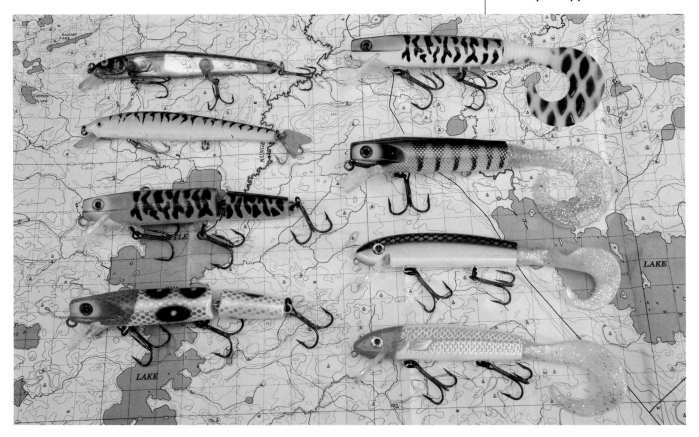

The last few years, we had good success with Stalkers and Super Stalkers, and last year I really nailed them with the new small-size Squirrely Jake. The key is something that can be retrieved erratically and be cast a long distance. Heavy spoons are great here, too.

Early in the year, pike take a toll on spawning suckers. But once it gets hot outside, walleyes become one of the main choices on the pikes' menu. When water temperatures reach 65 degrees, if you find walleyes, chances are very good that pike are somewhere nearby. Wind-blown rocky points are a great place to find pike feeding on walleyes at this time. Casting to these spots can be very productive at times, but there are other approaches as well. Trolling crankbaits and drift jigging are both efficient presentations, and are a good way to cover the entire point.

Let's take a look at trolling first. Imagine a rocky point off the end of an island. It is a long point, running out into the main lake, and gets progressively deeper the further from the island you go. Deeper-diving crankbaits are the choice here. So let's say you have a Squirrely Li'l Ernie on, and your partner has an 8-inch Believer. As you approach the upper end of the point, both you and your partner can feel those lures bouncing off the rocks as they climb up the side of the point. Then, as you pass over the top, you feel the lure break free and as you continue on, you feel it working its way down the other side.

A couple of large jigs for drifting across rocky points, and two trolling choices: Li'l Ernie and a Squirrely Li'l Ernie. MIKE TRETTIN

Many times the hit will come just as you break free from the top of the point. Barring a hit, you keep moving along, and once your lure quits contacting rocks, you make a wide swing and head back to the point to give the opposite side the same treatment. By doing this, you can make adjustments to every pass and work your way down the entire length of the point. If you make contact, you will want to make several passes over that same spot. The main criteria for a good crankbait with which to troll points are the ability to dive deep, and the ability to take the punishment of bouncing off rocks. Those rocks can beat a lesser crankbait into submission. If you have a floating crankbait that sinks, change it. It has developed a leak and is filling with water; this will ruin its action quickly.

Drift jigging is another very effective technique. When drift jigging, you are, of course, at the mercy of the wind as far as direction goes. However, the motor can be used for adjustments. Heavy jigs dressed with large plastic trailers are going to be your bait of choice here. Reapers (resembling an eel), lizards, and large curly-tailed grubs all work well. Another good option is a heavy, plain, short-armed spinnerbait tipped with either a large minnow, a small sucker, or a river chub.

Let's imagine that same long point. The wind is blowing across the point, making it ideal to drift across. You motor to the upwind side and check the waves to pick a lane through which to drift. Turning the boat sideways, you lower the jig to the bottom and begin to drift, jigging straight down over the side of the boat. With a heavier jig, it is easy to keep the line fairly vertical. This is important to keep snagging in the rocks to a minimum. As the boat nears the point and the depths get shallower, you will have to shorten the amount of line you have out to maintain this near-vertical line. As you crest the top and depths start to increase again, you will have to lengthen the line to maintain contact with the bottom.

At times, a sharp snap, lifting the jig two or three feet off the bottom, is best. Other times, a slow lift-and-lower technique, occasionally ticking the bottom, will work best. Experimentation will reveal which is better on a given day.

How heavy a jig to use will depend on how hard the wind is blowing. The stronger the wind, the faster your boat will drift and the heavier a jig you will need to keep that line nearly vertical. A drift sock can be used to help slow the drift, but unless the wind is really howling, I don't bother with one. I'm looking for aggressive feeders here, and they don't mind chasing their prey a bit.

After you have made your initial drift, motor back upwind and try to place the boat in a different lane, where you will drift over the point just a little deeper. By repeating this process, you will be able to cover the entire length of the point.

When there is a change in wind direction, the pike will gradually move to different locations. Sometimes it is just a matter of repositioning on the same point, and other times it may mean a move to a different point. Wherever those walleyes go, the pike are sure to follow. This is an easy area to identify, and can be quickly checked for aggressive pike. Another bonus is the inevitable capture of walleyes for a tasty shore lunch.

Trolling the Breaklines

Trolling breaklines (locations with depth changes, also called dropoffs) during the hot summer is a great method for targeting those pike that roam the open waters. Large schools of whitefish and ciscoes roam these same waters, often along these breaklines, and provide pike with plenty of nourishment.

We use some specialized equipment to go after these wanderers. There are a couple of books on the market on trolling that are of great benefit to the long-line troller. (They are *Precision Trolling: The Troller's Bible* by Mark Romanack and *Precision Trolling* by Steven Holt.) These books feature detailed diving curves for a great many lures. When you couple the information in the book with a good line-counter reel and a lake map showing depths, you can keep your lure precisely where it needs to be.

Let's look at a typical scenario. Checking the map, you will notice contour lines showing depths. Look down the shoreline into which the wind is blowing and search for the 20-foot line. This is where I like to start. I make my trolling runs in a lazy S-shaped path, weaving in and out between the 20- and 30-foot marks. Now, checking one of those precision-trolling books, I find that a Bomber Long Deep Diver, model 25A, will dive to 20 feet with 68 feet of line out. And if I need to go deeper, 120 feet of line will get me down to 26 feet, and with 195 feet of line it will go down to 30 feet. These depths are calibrated using a line with the same diameter as 10-pound monofilament.

Locations in Rivers

Rivers do not get as warm as lakes, due to their continually moving current. They also differ in that lakes generally have a wider variety of habitat. They are similar, however, in that any resident pike will move to seek preferred temperature ranges.

Incoming creeks are usually pike magnets. The added current helps to keep temperatures down and oxygenate the water. And baitfish will gather where creeks run into a river. Crankbaits work well in these areas. A shallow runner is preferred to keep the bait from digging into the bottom where snagging could be a problem. I like one that has a long and narrowed body, with a tight wiggle, like a number 18 Rapala or the Bomber Mag Long A. Anchor upstream and slightly out from the creek entrance, and fan-cast the entire area, pulling the crankbait back upstream. Try several types of retrieves, all the way from a very erratic jerky retrieve to just swimming it straight in.

Trees lying in the water are key spots to check in a river. CRYSTAL PANFILL

Swimming jigs are another option. A long twister tail grub from 4 to 6 inches works well. I like yellow, white, and black, in that order. Most of the time, a simple, straight retrieve works well with these. That tail fluttering around is enough to trigger aggressive fish. If the incoming creek is large enough, a large, long hole may have formed in the riverbed. If nothing happens after you swim a jig through the hole a few times, try hopping one off the bottom of that hole. Drifting the length of these holes with swimming jigs has also proven to be very effective.

Inline spinners might just be the best bet where these creeks enter a river. The number-5 Mepps, or a number-5 or -6 Blue Fox, are all good choices. Even some of the smaller muskie bucktails work well. Choose bright colors like white, chartreuse, yellow, or orange to begin with. Then black, with either a metallic or red blade, would be a good option to try. A quicker retrieve works best most days.

Another spot to always check is trees blown down into the water. These create a current break, and pike will lie beside them to ambush prey swimming by.

The best pike location for rivers in summer has to be where a cold-water spring flows in. The fish often stack up in these places. The problem with springs is that they are hard to locate, and the best way I know how is to spot them in winter. While the rest of the area is frozen, the spot where the spring is located will still be open. I make mental notes of these spots for future use in open water.

CHAPTER SEVEN

Fall

Temperature range: 40 to 60 degrees

As the air starts to become crisp, the knowledgeable pike fisherman starts rubbing his hands together in anticipation. Fall is when the real big girls come to dance. This is the time when pike go all out, feeding heavily and getting ready for the onslaught of winter. For me, it has meant not only my best pike day ever (with nine pike over twenty pounds), but also accounted for the three biggest pike I've ever caught. By the time October rolls around, skinny pike are rare. This is the season of the heavyweights.

Locations in Lakes

Weeds

As the season changes and water temperatures begin to fall, the pike will once again start to change locations. The fish living at the bottom of those thick cabbage beds are facing a changing environment as the weeds start to turn brown and die. Green weeds give off oxygen and keep the area breathable; dead brown weeds do not. This die-off is a gradual one, and the pike will move to the areas within the weed bed that contain the greenest weeds. What this means for us is that the big pike congregate in areas of continually smaller size. This does not mean that big pike cannot be caught out of brown weeds, but they won't remain there long.

There are several options available in lure choice, many of which we've already discussed. Spinnerbaits fished deep are a good start. If you have access to natural bait, a plain, short-armed spinnerbait tipped with a large minnow, chub, or small sucker can be the best possible offering. I also like to use a willow-bladed one with bright colors here, but as always, be versatile. Spoons are another productive lure. We've done well casting the larger Eppinger Troll Devles, and others of equal sizes in the fall period. But there are a couple of other lures I haven't covered very much yet that really shine here.

The first lures I'd like to discuss are jerkbaits. Basically, there are two types: those that dive and rise, and the gliders. Both will work well here, but I prefer the gliders in this instance. As we discussed earlier, gliders have no action of their own. If retrieved steadily, they will just pull straight in. It is up to the angler to impart action into these lures.

Cast the lure out and reel in the slack line. With the rod tip pointed down, give the lure a downward jerk of about twelve to twenty-four inches and the lure will dive, glide to the side, and pause. Quickly reel in most (but not all) of the slack line, and jerk again. Leaving just a small amount of slack before repeating the jerk will create a snap, and will turn the bait in the opposite direction. You must pay close attention to the amount of slack because if there is too much, you won't be able to get a good hook set in the event of a strike or be able to get the proper jerk on the lure. If there is no slack, your lure won't get the proper action.

Usually, pike will hit the bait at the end of the glide, during the short pause. However, be vigilant in watching the line and lure, as fish may hit it when it changes direction or during the glide. Sometimes it helps to mix up the retrieve a bit. Instead of a big jerk, try a couple of short taps and then the jerk. Or a tap, jerk, pause; tap, tap, jerk, pause; tap, jerk, pause . . . You get the idea. Just mix it up and experiment. The pike will let you know which they like best.

My personal favorite gliders include the Eddie Bait and the Magic Maker. The Magic Maker is an unusual jerkbait in that you can actually get good action out of it with just the reel by turning the handle quickly one

Top to bottom: a "glider," Eddie Bait, and Magic Maker. MIKE TRETTIN

turn at a time. It won't get the long glide that way, but sometimes that is not the key. Some gliders are weighted so they rise much more slowly, if at all, keeping them in the pike's strike zone longer. A high-speed reel is required with any of these lures to quickly pick up the slack line. And a heavy-action rod is needed, as these lures typically weigh 2 ounces and up.

The dive-and-rise-type jerkbaits have a design that causes them to dive and then float back to the surface. At times, these will produce very well. The Suick is the most well-known, and for good reason: They are very productive lures. Several sizes are available, and I've done well with all of them. When fishing lake weeds, I choose a larger size.

There is another lure that combines the actions of a glider and a dive-and-rise. The Burt by Muskie Mania Tackle will dive, but when it reaches its maximum depth, it will swing out to the side, then rise. It also comes in weighted models that will not rise nearly as far as the unweighted models.

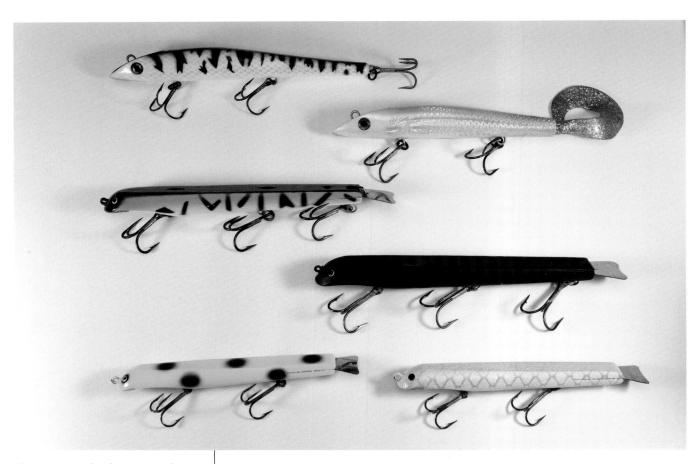

The Burt, Squirrely Burt, and Suicks (bottom four lures) are all excellent dive-and-rise jerkbaits.
MIKE TRETTIN

The Squirrely Burt is the same lure, but the tail end has been removed and replaced with a wide twister tail. In my experience, this addition makes it nearly twice as effective, although the plain versions work well, too.

Another very productive lure here is the jig. The jigs we used on the sand flats earlier in the year, like the Esox Cobra Jig, will work well here dressed with a rubber trailer. Another one I like is made by High Roller Lures, and features a head that looks realistic and a body with a paddle tail. The whole thing resembles a baitfish very closely, and is quite effective.

Quite a few jigs will work well here. Some will be better on a given day than others, so I find it best to carry several different types and let the pike tell me what they like. Jigs with a twister tail, a reaper or a split-tail eel, a lizard or a tube—they all have their days. And then there are hair jigs. Hair jigs are just what the name implies—jigs made with hair trailers. I have seen various forms of hair used for these, including polar bear hair used on jigs in northern Canada. But the most common material is deer hair, also known as bucktail. These have been in use for a long time and are still productive, especially when used for this pattern. Bucktail jigs seem to

Bucktail jig, High Roller jig, and Esox Cobra jigs with a twister tail and Reaper. JACK PENNY

sink faster than jigs dressed with rubber, and the hair acts much differently with a more fluid motion to it. My favorite way to fish any of these jigs in the dying weeds is to cast one out and let it sink. As soon as I feel it contact the weeds, I snap it upward quickly and let it sink again. When you are retrieving through the dying weeds, it is simple to rip it out and through them without hanging up much.

Rocks

Another location in the fall involves rocks. Whitefish and ciscoes spawn in the fall on gravelly or rocky bottoms, and the pike will show up in huge numbers to feed on them. This could be at the mouths of incoming streams, the tops of reefs, or just gravelly shallows. Depths are usually from three to ten feet. These spawning species will show up in large numbers to propagate, and present excellent feeding opportunities for pike. These species exhibit silvery sides, so a crankbait that is silvery and flashy will be the best offering here. A Super Shad Rap even has a similar profile and is an excellent choice. We've also done well with Stalkers, both jointed and

A shoreline featuring a gravel bottom. Ciscoes and whitefish spawn in areas like this in late fall. JACK PENNY

Opposite: Fish these baits high in the water column, with a quick retrieve for an aggressive fall presentation. MIKE TRETTIN

straight. The idea is to use something that is flashy and doesn't dive too deep. A Believer tied on the shallower eyelet has worked well too. Large flashy spoons are likewise a very good choice.

Locations in Rivers

Fall pike fishing on rivers is largely overlooked, and this presents a two-sided coin. On one side, it is great for those in the know who have this great fishing all to themselves. On the other side of the coin, too bad for those who don't know about it. They don't know what they are missing.

The pike here, like their lake-dwelling brethren, are also building up body reserves for the upcoming winter, and are at their maximum weight of the year. This means that their metabolism is in high gear and they are, for

Casting to current breaks below a dam in late fall. JACK PENNY

the most part, very active. For this reason, when I start fishing a particular location, I start with an aggressive presentation. I want something that moves water and is flashy, and nothing fits the bill better than a spinnerbait or a spinner.

I like to use a heavier spinnerbait here, like a ¾- or 1-ounce model with large Colorado blades. I'm not concerned that the lure is going to run too deep, because I'm going to use a quick retrieve. I want the lure to run just below the surface of the water. Normally, the pike will smash it, but if not, I'll try bringing it in a couple of feet below the surface. The same goes for the inline spinner—lots of flash and a quick retrieve. But it doesn't necessarily have to be one of the bladed baits. As always, a good strategy is for each angler in the boat to cast a different offering until a pattern is established. Flashy spoons or crankbaits can also produce very well.

Incoming creeks are again a key spot, no matter how small they may be. In the fall period, while the main river cools down, this incoming water will be slightly warmer and will attract all species of fish, thus kicking the food chain into gear. After working the area over with spinnerbaits and spinners, I like to make several casts with something a bit more subtle, like a brightly colored Slug-Go. An erratic retrieve will usually put a few more in the boat before I move on.

Another key location is below dams. Perch and walleye migrate upstream at this time, and pike are sure to follow. Try casting to current breaks and retrieve upstream. Pike will stage just off to the side of current areas and wait for prey to pass by. Lures will be about the same here as they were at incoming water. Flashy is the best way to start.

CHAPTER EIGHT

Winter

Temperature range: Below 40 degrees

The Hardwater Season

Pike fishing through the ice is probably nearly as old as the existence of man. Tribes in the far north have been spearing pike through the ice seemingly forever. Because I am concerned with protecting pike and encouraging catch and release, I will not focus on spear fishing in this book, other than to use it as an example of how far back the history of ice fishing goes. This is a popular sport that is enjoyed around the northern parts of the world. People in Canada and all the way to Germany, Sweden, Russia, Norway, and Finland enjoy catching pike through the ice. Here in the United States, the entire northern tier of states from Idaho to New York offer good opportunities, as does Alaska.

Any time ice fishing is being discussed, personal safety must be a concern. I've listed the things I consider most important below.

1. Never go alone, and tell someone where you're going.
2. Wear a personal flotation device.

3. Walk in single file, with one angler following the other and spaced apart.

4. If you are using a sled to transport gear, tie a long rope to it. The sled will pull more easily and in the event someone falls through, the sled can be pushed to them while holding onto the rope.

5. Always carry a throwable boat cushion. I tie a long rope to this also. If you elect to tie a rope to it, be sure to wrap the rope all the way around the cushion and tie a tight knot. If you tie to the handle on the cushion, it will rip out.

6. Keep the "spikes of life" around your neck. These are spikes protruding out of two handles, and are used to pull your way onto solid ice if you happen to break through the ice. Once you've pulled yourself out, do not stand up. Instead, roll across the ice in the direction from which you came until you are sure you're over safe ice.

7. Keep the auger blades covered to prevent cuts.

8. Wear spikes on your boots to avoid slipping and falling on the ice. There are several good ones available that slip on over your boots.

9. Before going out, spray your auger blades and boots with a nonstick cooking spray, such as Pam. The snow won't stick, so you won't be hauling around pounds of it on your boots and you won't get cut cleaning off the blades.

The first thing to be concerned with is how thick the ice is and whether it will support your weight. Good guidelines are:

4 inches—200 pounds, or one person with gear
5 inches—800 pounds, or one snowmobile
7 inches—1,500 pounds, or a group of people
8 inches—2,000 pounds, or one car
12 inches—small truck

Be aware that ice may not be the same thickness all over, and stay clear of anything sticking up through the ice like trees, logs, plants, or even docks. Ice fishing on rivers usually means taking unnecessary chances with your life, and my best advice would be to avoid it entirely. Moving current eats away at ice from underneath. The ice could be a foot thick in one spot and only a couple of inches thick just a few feet away. And if you fall through the ice, there is a good chance that the moving current will pull you under the surface. Risking death for a fish is a poor bargain.

Equipment

The popularity of ice fishing has grown tremendously in recent years. Many manufacturers have followed suit, and there is now a wide array of items specifically designed for the ice fishing crowd. There are specially designed clothes to keep the cold out, and portable shelters so you can sit comfortably in warmth. The day of the plain jigging rod is nearly over, as there are now species-specific rods and reels. And the electronics available now are unbelievable. There are all kinds of flashers and liquid crystal graphs for use on the ice.

As for depth-finding, for years the clip-on heavy weights that one attaches to the line worked fine for me, but using them is slow and you must cut holes first before finding depth. I now use a flasher made by Vexilar. I can see the bottom depth without drilling, as long as I clear away the snow and add a little water to the surface of the ice. A flasher will tell you anything any other depth finder will, if you know how to interpret the information it sends. The Vexilar flashers' signals are shown in three separate colors, and will indicate not only the bottom composition but also fish size. Lower your bait close to the transducer and you can watch it fall all the way to the bottom. If a fish comes in but is higher up than your bait sits, you will see it and can simply raise the bait up to the desired level.

I now also use a handheld GPS. The unit I have has a feature that mostly overrides the required satellite inaccuracy for Homeland Security reasons. It claims to be accurate to nine feet and seems even better than that. So I punched in waypoints on my favorite pike lakes during the open water season, and walk right to them on the hardwater, saving lots of time compared to the old days.

The most intriguing of all the new inventions used in ice fishing has to be the underwater camera. You can learn so much by watching that camera screen. You get to see exactly how fish react to different presentations and how they relate to structure. I've spent hours with my eyes glued to that viewer and have learned many things I hadn't previously known, and have also been able to eliminate some ideas I had that proved to be false. These cameras would benefit anyone. The most well-known and the only one I've personally tried is the Aqua-Vu, but there are others available. Some folks might say that all these inventions have given the angler an unfair advantage. I heard the same arguments when graphs first hit the market. Remember, however: Just because you can see a fish doesn't mean you can make it bite.

Ice fishing for northern pike is a whole new ball game, compared to fishing the rest of the year. You now must target very specific spots instead of covering a fifty-yard swath with each cast. There will be days when your bait barely reaches bottom before getting bit. There will also be days when the exact opposite is true, and no matter what you do, they just won't bite. But, some very big pike come through the hole every year and every one I've seen looked very well fed. I recall reading at least one study which showed that pike displayed significant growth in winter, whereas all other species in the study did not. As part of that picture, however, this is cold water and a pike's metabolism is low, so its feeding needs are reduced. In other words, pike will feed heavily at times, but they don't need to do it nearly as often.

In many areas, ice fishing for pike is a social event. On larger lakes, roads are plowed and even stop signs are in place. Fish shacks dot the frozen landscape and it is a small city out there. While this is fun, I prefer a more mobile approach while still retaining the camaraderie. I personally like going out with a group of guys, setting up on some structure with tip-ups, and socializing. A grill with bratwurst, or a stove and a pot of chili, coupled with some beverages, makes for a fun afternoon. And if the fish are too slow in coming, it is easy to move.

Winter Pike Location

Like any other season, winter pike angling starts with trying to fish where the fish are. While most of us approach our favorite pike lake and determine where to begin fishing, more thought should first be given to selecting the lake itself. As is the case any time of year, it's partly a matter of individual angler preference, usually a trade-off between population density and quality. Some will gladly fish days on end for one strike from a big fish, while others want lots of action, even if the fish are small. But for most of us, what's probably best is a decent compromise in the form of good numbers and size potential; not waiting forever between strikes, but also not a situation where frequent action seems to practically guarantee only small fish.

Whatever your priorities, also consider the characteristics of the lake. Some very productive open-water lakes are much tougher in the winter for complex reasons, stemming from structure or lack thereof, weed growth, and other factors. Fortunately, a few lakes are the opposite; pike are actually easier to pattern in winter. It's been my experience that lakes with limited structure and sparse weeds (or those that seem to die off and disappear quickly in late fall), and/or lakes with very abundant forage, tend to present more difficult fishing in winter. Success is generally higher on lakes where fish can be better located by targeting well-defined structure or at least some remnant vegetation, and are relatively receptive to easy meals due to not having an overabundance of food sources.

As far as where to start your efforts on your chosen lake, popular theory suggests shallow bays and structures on early season ice, deeper areas in midwinter (even similar to midsummer locales), and shallower again on late ice, near spawning locations where pike might be staging then. This way of thinking is not a bad start on many waters, though it really all depends on where the food is. On many lakes, very late fall finds prey and predators quite deep, and this may or may not continue on early winter ice.

Other lakes (let's say those that are characterized by typical deep summer fish) experience forage movements that keep fish shallow all winter. One of my favorite lakes displays this pattern, but another is just the opposite; pike in winter there are deeper than the rest of the year. I am unaware of any formula that can predict which way it will go; it simply boils down to spending plenty of time on the ice and developing your best informed guesswork. Fortunately, however, when you do identify the trends on a particular lake, they seem to continue winter after winter.

Because there are no easy shortcuts, as mentioned, it always pays to know as much as you can about forage types and their relative distributions on your chosen venues. Perch as a major food source can lead to pike quite deep in midwinter, but not always. Other panfish like bluegill and crappie are oftentimes active and shallower very early and late in the day. Where this happens, the pike are not far behind if those species are their major food source. Find out all you can about where and when the panfish anglers are having the most success. They probably won't appreciate you setting tip-ups right next to them, but doing so at a discreet distance or at other similar areas is usually a good bet.

Fortunately, prey species tend to collect in classic places like inside turns on a dropoff, especially with remaining weeds (alive or dead) around. This is in fact my favorite winter type of spot, and the tighter and more defined, the better. Fish have never been taught that dead weeds are a bad thing anyway, contrary to some popular thinking. Much of the time the green stuff is not there or you can't find it, and even dead cover to hold prey is a lot better than nothing. It's well worth the extra effort to try snagging up some vegetation with a heavy treble dropped to the bottom through your holes.

Other typical pike structures besides inside turns are sometimes worthy, like points, which can have at least gradual inside turns adjacent to them worth trying, too. On lakes without much variety to their contours, I still prefer to work the most well-defined dropoffs that can be found, ideally with old weeds on them. Some, or even most, fish may be scattered all over the flats above the drop at any given time, but they are difficult to find with the proverbial needle-in-the-haystack approach that tip-ups or vertical jigging really are, even if you move them a lot (one exception being an isolated, thick patch of weeds). Usually fish will still gravitate toward that edge at some point, though, so working baits up on it where the flat starts, down it partway, and down deep, all have their place at times. That's why at least three holes per line are recommended as a bare minimum, many more if practical, to keep moving baits around. (More on this later.)

One piece of advice a good ice angler showed me is to set a tip-up just off the edge of a steep drop, yet with the bait set shallow; say, just three feet down over fifteen feet of water. The goal is for it to be seen, both by cruising fish down below as well as fish up on the shallow flat, if visibility is good. I've had some luck with this approach in the right situations.

Strategies and Tactics

Preparation

Obviously, the equipment list for pike fishing through the ice will read much differently than the lists from previous periods. The quick-strike rigs do not differ much from what I use for deadbaiting in the spring, but that is virtually the only thing in common with open-water tackle.

Take the common tip-up, for example. It consists of a wooden or plastic frame with a metal rod that pivots and contains a reel on one end, and a flag mounted on another rod that is attached to a spring on the base. The reel sits below the water's surface with the frame straddling the hole. On the opposite end of the rod containing the reel is a cross bar under which the flag rests. When a fish takes the bait, the rod revolves and the flag is released, giving you the signal that a fish is on the run.

These things have been around a very long time, and are still the favorites of many. There are many manufacturers offering tip-ups, and with the recent wave of popularity to the sport, there are new ones on the market every year. Frabill makes a neat one called the Pro Thermal, which is a round plastic affair that sits on top of and covers the hole completely. With the warmth from the sun, it will keep the hole ice-free for the most part. They fit nicely in a five-gallon bucket, making transportation of several a tangle-free ordeal.

Many may laugh at the use of hole covers if they are not already part of your tip-up. I used to as well, but then became a believer. This is not only because of their ability to block out light for a more natural presentation, but more importantly they prevent or slow the hole-freezing process. An inexpensive alternative cover consists of an old black rubber floor mat cut into squares that cover the holes, with slots cut to fit in the tip-up. These work very well, and the black rubber material attracts plenty of warmth to keep the holes relatively ice-free on most days.

A hole cover made from a black rubber floor mat. JOE BEDNAR

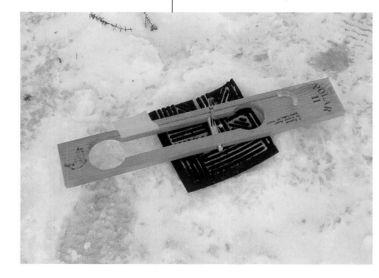

As in all types of fishing, careful thought beforehand is important. I'll go over some particulars focusing on tip-up fishing, including

MUST-HAVE LIST

Auger

Spoon to clear ice debris from holes

Tip-ups rigged and ready, with at least one extra per angler

Hole covers, if not already part of the tip-up

Insulated minnow bucket and scooping net (hint: tie the net to the bucket to avoid forgetting it)

Bait prepared as desired

Handheld GPS

Depth finder

Aqua-Vu camera (optional, but very handy and educational)

what to bring with you and what to bring on you, which are included in the lists accompanying this chapter. Note that the lists include what is most important for the fishing part of the experience, and omit clothing, food, beverage, and other essentials out of the scope of this discussion and entirely up to you and your common sense.

Tip-ups loaded with appropriate line (I use braided lines) and well-maintained leaders are obvious, and the extra tip-up per man is mentioned since it can be a big time-saver in resuming fishing after those times when a fish or mishap results in a completely or severely compromised tip-up. For leaders, I've been using the new softer type of wire like Surflon Micro Supreme, which can be tied into knots and wound right onto the little spool without problems. I make these leaders extra long, starting at 24 inches or more if not fishing very shallow, so as the hook end gets roughed up, I can retie several times instead of tossing the entire leader. Quick-strike rigs are usually the preferred hook arrangement for release fishing, though with any hook arrangement what's most important is not letting fish swallow baits deeply.

One tip I'd like to share is the use of bass-style, cone-shaped slip sinkers threaded on the line backwards above your leaders. They slip through old weed debris quite well, or slide up the line if they do hang on something when that pike is running with the bait, so fish are less likely to feel resistance and drop it. Another practice I believe in is marking the line in five-foot intervals on my tip-ups used for deeper waters. On black lines I find that a dab of red nail polish works pretty well for these marks, lasting at least a season or two. On green lines just use a black permanent marker to make the marks; it's easier and lasts indefinitely. This is a much better means of depth-marking than little floats, buttons or other signals affixed onto the line, which can catch on things just like firmly placed sinkers do.

Live bait should be acquired just before your outing if possible, but as a practical matter, this is sometimes the day before if you're getting a very early start in the morning, or several days when using bait from previous outings. If you can, it pays to prepare any bait before you go, such as the evening before. For me, this means trimming the tails on live baits to slow them down, or puncturing the air bladders on dead baits like smelt. These measures can save both time and freezing hands on the ice. For keeping live bait any longer than a few hours at home, always use an aerator, and pay attention to how cold or warm that water gets. If it gets too warm, those minnows are in trouble when they hit the cold water. My garage usually works well in all but the coldest weather, with the aerator helping to stir things up and slow ice formation.

As for the baits themselves, depending on where you fish, your live bait options are most likely suckers or shiners, or possibly chubs. Suckers are pretty lethargic on the hook after they settle down from the initial setup, but they are quite hardy, and their laziness can be appealing to lethargic winter pike. Shiners have more flash, but are quite fragile and don't last long if moving them around from hole to hole, especially in very cold temperatures. Chubs are the toughest of all; they might even try to fight back against an attacking pike. But they can be too active for slower-moving winter fish, so it's just as well that they aren't readily available in most areas.

You can't get any less active and easy to catch than a dead bait, which is no doubt a big part of why countless giant pike through the ice and open water have been caught on various dead bait offerings. I'll never forget the first time I used a dead smelt. I couldn't get whole versions anywhere in my home region, so I complained until a friend from Wisconsin sent me some frozen versions in the mail. Within five minutes the first tip-up with a smelt was attacked and that fat winter pike was screaming line off the spool like it had found the prize of its life. Needless to say, it left a lasting impression. I still can't get dead smelt easily, and usually just resort to deceased versions of the baits mentioned above.

In my view, the very best bait of all is one that is somewhere between live and dead, ideally a mortally wounded minnow that has been ravaged by a pike, or caught one yet you didn't lose the bait. It can't move quickly enough to escape anything, emits plenty of scent including panic pheromones (at least, so I'm told), yet does have a little movement to attract pike, unlike dead baits. It has the best of both worlds. In addition to the tail clipping mentioned previously, I've been known to mash the back ends of minnows with my boots, trying not to crush their organs and kill

PREPARATION TIPS

Use cone-shaped slip sinkers backwards.

Use long leaders if not fishing very shallow.

Mark lines in five-foot intervals for deep fishing.

Prepare bait before fishing when possible.

them, when the pike don't help me get mortally wounded minnows.

A couple items are mentioned separately because they must be on your person, so you don't have to go back to your sled or tackle bucket for them while unhooking and releasing fish. I'd say my biggest pet peeve on the ice, besides guys waiting too long to set hooks and otherwise killing fish in general, is guys leaving a pike flopping around, then freezing on the ice as they walk back for pliers or whatever else they need to unhook the fish. The most important aspect of catch and release is that any fish returned to the water is done so as quickly as possible, with as little ill effect on the fish as possible, no matter what its size.

Setting Up

Say there are two of you, and you've got the whole day set aside for fishing. I believe it pays to have everything ready and fishing before first light, since that is often the best time of the entire day. So be prepared to be setting up in the dark and also picking up in the dark, since evenings are another prime time.

In my opinion, it's important to drill all your holes beforehand in a given area so as to not disturb things while actually fishing. Consider it another way of trying to tip the odds in your favor as much as possible. With two guys, this means the first guy checks depths with the sonar unit and drills holes where desired, and the second guy clears them of ice debris, marks the depth next to them for reference later (if there's snow), and sets up the tip-ups in the holes selected for actual fishing. I use a motorized auger, and with this I like a minimum of three holes per tip-up: shallow, medium, and deep along a given contour for moving the tip-ups around while actually fishing. With all holes, it can help later to throw ice debris and slush upwind where it won't catch your line when dealing with fish later. Since this can make your extra holes tougher to find as the day wears on, especially on a windy day with blowing snow, use your boots to push up the slushy ice into a little wall upwind of the hole to act as a visual marker.

For two guys with two tip-ups allowed each, this means a total of at least twelve holes must be prepared for the four tip-ups to work a given area, though it's better to have twice that many or even more if the ice isn't too thick. This should not be too large an area either, since for release fishing you shouldn't be too far from those tip-ups and it lets you work a given area reasonably well with those twelve or more holes. Those who place a tip-up here and there acres and acres apart might never know if a given area around their tip-ups will produce, since that one line is less likely to intercept a fish than four lines moving around in twelve to twenty-four or more holes in an area that's not too large, but carefully chosen.

In waters up to ten or twelve feet deep or so, I usually start with the bait not more than halfway down so it's up where fish can see it, and even higher if old weeds require it (such as you might encounter on early ice), assuming water clarity is good where you're fishing. In deeper waters of fifteen feet or more, I usually start within two or three feet off the bottom. Deeper pike usually seem to feed closer to the bottom in winter, but if the presence of old weeds requires it I'll start higher up even in deeper waters. In all cases, err toward placing baits too high rather than too low. Better to let them at least see the bait rather than the bait getting down into old weeds or other cover. Remember that these recommendations are just a starting point. I, too, have been on waters where baits must be nearly on the bottom to get any action.

Ice-fishing bait on quick-strike rigs should be hooked differently than in many open-water applications, with the end hook near the middle of the bait and the second hook somewhere near the tail on a quick-strike. This lets live bait struggle to swim downward, toward the security of depth or cover, and with live or dead bait it helps reduce the number of deeply hooked fish since they tend to swallow bait head-first. You may have witnessed or read of anglers going to great lengths to hang dead bait as horizontally as possible, including such methods as inserting nails in them to weight them just right, but I truly believe a pike that's looking to eat could care less if that easy meal is horizontal or not, and leaving nails in released pike is irresponsible to say the least. Just hook them up like live

SETUP TIPS

Drill all holes before starting to fish an area.

Have extra holes for each tip-up.

Throw ice and slush upwind of the holes.

Push ice debris into walls to mark holes for later.

Mark the hole depth in the snow nearby for reference later.

Err toward placing baits higher in the water column.

bait, except you'll normally have to puncture the swim bladder so they sink.

Tip-Up Fishing Tips

This is the easy part, really, and probably doesn't require as much discussion as all the pre-fishing material. Now the waiting game starts, and the waiting can be as active or as passive as you like—although, as with the other steps, more effort usually pays off. I try not to let a tip-up set idle for more than fifteen or twenty minutes, maybe a half hour at the most, with the first check consisting of lifting the bait up to the surface and returning it, oftentimes with some jigging action before I leave it in place again.

This accomplishes at least three things. One, if a fish has been observing the minnow for a while, as pike often do in this situation, I believe the fish might realize that minnow will not stick around forever and occasionally will strike soon after the bait is returned. Second, the lift and drop, plus some jigging while you're at it, can help get that bait noticed in the first place by any pike in the area, plus distribute the scent of the bait more thoroughly. Third, if nothing else, you'll know the minnow is okay and not down too deep in weeds, twisted strangely on the hooks, or even wrapped around the tip-up reel somehow.

When nothing has happened to that particular tip-up after thirty or forty minutes, including the lift-and-drop drill a time or two, then it's time to move the bait to one of the pre-drilled backup holes. Sometimes I can't even wait that long, depending on how I feel in my gut about things that day. Then the process starts over. If you get a flag that is from a legitimate fish take, or better yet actually catch a pike, the process starts over right in that same hole, sticking with it a good while before even thinking about leaving it. On the tough days—and I've had plenty—one legitimate fish contact in a particular hole is oftentimes reason enough to work it the rest of that outing, using other lines for more exploring, including moving to the depth of the hole that got the action. Too many days I've seen all the action from just one or two holes, so you never want to abandon them too soon. If you must move after a while, I'd still recommend returning later to check things out again.

Now let's say our hardy pair of pikers has done all this, methodically checking each of the three holes per tip-up for a good while, and after about two hours things are still dead out there. It's time, or maybe past time, to move completely, and this presents what I believe are two options. One is picking up everything and starting in a totally different place on the lake, and the other is employing the "leapfrog" method of moving, if reasonably good water is adjacent to the area where you started. This approach is just like it sounds: starting with the first tip-up in the water that day, move it down the contour a ways and "leapfrog" it past the others, covering a whole new span of water by the time you move each tip-up. When doing this, I sometimes drop the drill-all-your-holes-first principle, just to spread out the tasks and alleviate the sheer boredom that can occur while fishing tip-ups on slow days. Plus, who knows? On the tough days when it seems the fish aren't moving, perhaps intermittent drilling along a given area can at least get them wandering a bit instead of just lying there all day with you hoping to accidentally drop a bait on their noses.

Finally, a little advice on actually catching the fish. Move to a tripped tip-up quickly, but don't sprint, as that can alert the fish depending on ice thickness and their mood that day. A rapid yet quiet walk is about right. Set the hook right away as well—that fish either has it or it doesn't, and more delay can just give more time for the fish to drop the bait altogether. You may miss one now and then, but they'll live, which is more than can be said for fish permitted to take the bait way down and then released after what is often a gruesome unhooking process. Most of the time you'll get them, and all it takes is a firm pulling up of the slack. Remember, you have no rod to absorb shock, and braided line with a wire leader has virtually no stretch. If the line is flying off the spool when you go to set, gently brake it to a stop with a gloved hand. This gets them practically every time.

Be firm, yet patient with the battle itself, always ready to use your fingers as a drag when that fish pulls hard. That happens at the start of the fight, almost any time during it, and near the hole about every time, so be ready. Try to lay out the line you've taken loosely and downwind, so your back should be facing upwind. Have your partner help keep that line laid out nice and available to feed back cleanly if it's a better fish, which also helps for winding it back on the spool afterwards.

Getting the fish through the hole itself is the trickiest part with a good-sized fish. Many times they'll pass under the hole several times. You have to pick the right time to get that head up in there and get a hand under the gill cover. After the fish is out of the hole, it's a matter of handling and unhooking the fish as carefully as any other time, but with time out of the water more critical on the coldest of days. At least the cold water helps greatly with survival odds, with winter-released pike demonstrating the lowest post-release mortality of any time during the year. Still, it is best to return the pike as quickly as possible, and always put them into the hole headfirst.

The older I get, the more I've come to appreciate the warmth of fishing in a shack, and the new portable models make it possible to move several times during the day with a minimum of effort. With some models, it is only a matter of flipping a folded top over a frame built on a plastic sled and drilling a hole, and you're in business. A simple Coleman lantern will heat it up fine on all but the coldest days. These shelters come in several sizes, from ones made for a single fisherman to ones that almost resemble a cabin. Want fresh hot coffee or lunch while you're out on the ice? A small cook stove will not only cook, it also helps heat up the shelter. One word of caution, though. If you're heating up or cooking in one of these huts, keep some ventilation vents open.

When sitting in the warmth of a shelter, I like to jig using a rod and reel. The rods are much shorter and reels are smaller. For pike, you'll want a rod that features plenty of backbone. The reels are comparable in size to a small walleye reel. I fill mine with 20-pound Fireline. Normally, I use a walleye jig and a float. I like a ¼-ounce jig, and attach a wire to the eye with a stinger treble on the end, much like the rig I use below floats at ice-out time in Ontario. A glowing jig head will often result in success far above what you would have without it.

I went ice fishing recently with a guy who really had all the details dialed in. He used an Aqua-Vu camera that had multiple lenses you could set in different directions. He would set up his tip-up outside the shelter and use a jigging rod inside. He could then send his camera lens down a separate hole to show both the bait on the tip-up and the jig on his rod and it would show both simultaneously on the viewer. If a pike nosed up to the bait on the tip-up, he saw it and was outside in a flash, waiting for the flag to spring. And if he saw one watching the jig, he would reach down and jig it slightly a couple of times and then let it sit motionless. When the pike grabbed it, he would quickly grab the rod from its holder and set the hook. A very efficient approach, to be sure.

At this point, I should explain about the rod holder. Most times, it will be best to put your rod in some kind of holder to avoid too much action getting imparted to the bait inadvertently. Pike will often sit and stare at a bait for a long time before hitting it. Too much jigging will turn them off. A better approach is to let it sit motionless and every once in a while jig it a couple of times, then let it sit still again. I've watched pike through the camera that sat and stared at the bait for a long time. When I jigged the bait just a couple of times and let it sit again, it wasn't long before they slid up and bit it. I like a rod holder that attaches to the rim of a five-gallon bucket and will position it so the rod tip is directly above the hole. With this setup, if I want to jig the bait a couple of times, I can simply reach over and tap the rod lightly with my hand and keep an eye on it closely. When the float starts to move down, I grab the rod and set the hook.

A Possible Winter Alternative

By late fall or early winter it's easy to get an empty or even downright depressed feeling, knowing that the open-water season is coming to a close, no matter how much you might like ice fishing. For me, it was always especially disheartening since at my latitude, ice formation is typically iffy and it can be January before I even get out. So in recent years I've been extending my late fall season into December, even into early January like last year, by making late fall/early winter pike trips on rivers with open water, and have had good results.

There are any number of rivers across the northern pike's range to try a late season float, with climatic aspects most favorable in places like the southern portions of Minnesota, Wisconsin, Michigan, and New York. I'd recommend sticking with an easily navigable stream. Early winter is no time to be dragging over logs or rocks likely to be covered in snow or ice. It's also a time to avoid getting hung up in deadfalls, so wider and slower is better than faster and narrower, even though the latter can make pike location more predictable. For the sake of safety, it is best to take an able-bodied companion along on winter river fishing or float trips. If possible, take two vehicles and park one at the launching point and the other at the finish spot. There are a lot of things that can go wrong and sometimes it is difficult to get back upstream, even when everything is seemingly fine.

One specific warning about personal safety: If you're in a small johnboat, as many are at this time and place, be aware of ice forming on the floor of the boat. A good friend nearly knocked himself out when he slipped during a hook set and cracked the back of his head on a bench in the boat. This could have been very serious, as he was fishing alone.

It's widely accepted that river predators gravitate toward deep holes sometime in the fall, and generally stay in these areas until spring; pike are no exception to this trend. Indeed, these holes are good bets for pike almost any time of year. However, I have encountered enough cold-weather pike holding in other river areas to warrant that efforts not be limited to just the deep holes. The one common denominator in cold weather has been slack water, as slow or still as can be found in the system. So in addition to deep, slow holes or pools, wide areas of the river that are slow but not deep can have at least a few fish at times, as can calm backwaters, even if very shallow.

Weather is of course critical, more so than at other times of the year. I don't push it if high temperatures for the day are below freezing. Warming trends are much better, and like in early spring, sunny afternoons are tops. Mornings can be very tough. I've gone all morning without enticing any interest, and then ended up having a good day with everything happening just in mid- to late afternoon.

Presentations for river pike very late in the season are the same or similar to what you'd expect in any colder-water situation. Slower retrieves with suspending jerkbaits are a primary pattern; slow-rolling spinnerbaits through deeper wood, lighter spoons with good action at low speed, jigs and plastics . . . you know the drill. As in other seasons, I find it pays to have a throwback offering rigged and ready. In this case, it will always be something slow and subtle. Something along the lines of a soft plastic jerkbait, or a jig and some kind of trailer, will do the trick.

Live and dead baits will also have their days in this period. Slowly floating a bait through a deep hole can be irresistible to a hungry pike. Even pike just lying there without a feeding urge will not pass up the opportunity if it drifts right to them. The rig we discussed in the ice-out chapter that utilizes a floating jig head works great here, too, when the boat is anchored upstream and the bait is placed on the rim of the hole.

CHAPTER NINE

Lure Modifications

Most of the lures you buy will catch pike at one time or another. Being the tinkering type, I'm seldom satisfied with many of them, and over time I have found modifications that I believe improve their performance. In this chapter, I will show you some of the tricks you can easily do to make your lures more effective.

Spoon Modifications

Spoons probably account for more pike caught than any lure out there. That could be because they are used more than any other lure. People, myself included, just plain love to fish spoons, and it is easy to see why. They are nearly indestructible, they don't develop leaks, and they do not need to be tuned. In fact, about the only maintenance involved is sharpening the hooks. And the only thing that may make them less effective is the loss of paint, but repainting is always possible. On top of all that, they can be used in just about any location or situation. Best of all though, is that pike bite them readily.

I modify my spoons in several ways that I believe add to the total catch. To start, I add a split ring to the front of the spoon if it doesn't already have one. I think it may add to the action of the spoon, and definitely makes changing them easier.

Another simple modification concerns the hooks. I almost always change from the treble hook to a single one. You will pick up a lot fewer weeds with a single hook. Weeds slide off them most times with just a jerk of the rod during your retrieve, and less weedy stuff means more fish. And you will hook those fish, too. I haven't noticed a significant drop in the number of pike I successfully hook up when using a single hook rather than the treble. The important thing about adding single hooks is to use the correct size. It is simple to determine which size to use by laying the hook against the back side of the spoon. You want the hook to reach close to both edges of the spoon without going past. Personally, I use the siwash style of hook that salmon fishermen use, but about any straight-shanked hook will work as long as it is strong. When changing to a single hook, be sure the hook point rides to the inside of the spoon.

The addition of trailers to spoons is something I consider to be very important. Every spoon I cast will have something attached to its rear. Weedless spoons work much better with soft plastic trailers added. We have been using Berkeley Power Grubs ever since they first came out to adorn our weedless spoons. I normally use the 1⅛-ounce size for Johnson Silver Minnows, with a 4-inch Power Grub that has been reduced in size. This has proven to be very effective. I also like a twin-tailed grub and a split-tailed eel on them. Those twin appendages look like legs kicking through the water, and have accounted for boatloads of big pike for us. Another great trailer for these spoons is one that the salmon guys call a hoochie. It has the appearance of a squid and comes in a variety of colors. Pike love them, and another bonus is that they won't slide down the hook as grubs tend to. One negative aspect of weedless spoons has to do with the hook on them. These spoons are assembled with the hook welded to the body of the spoon, and are then plated. This plating covers the spoon and the hook, and therein lies the problem. That plating on the hook makes it extremely dull. They must be sharpened before being used, and require touch-ups often.

I also use grubs to tip spoons like the Dardevle, but have a couple of other trailers that work very well, too. The first one is nothing but a simple little piece of red plastic shaped like a fish tail. To this day, I am amazed by how much difference this little piece of plastic makes. All that is required to add these is threading it onto the split ring holding the hook. I have also used a small Colorado blade in this manner and they add to it, too. But given the choice, I'd go with the plastic tail.

Probably my favorite trailer to add to these types of spoons is a small amount of spinnerbait-skirting material. Just a few strands will do it. If too much is added, it affects the action of the spoon. I use a skirt-making kit and make my own skirts to use on spoons. This kit consists of a special pair of pliers to hold the band, some skirt material, and some bands. I like to pull a few strands of the skirt through the hook eye until it is even on both sides, then take the pliers with the band attached, put it over the eye and down onto the shaft, stretching the skirting tight. Now, release the pliers and remove them, trim the material ends, and there you have it, a dressed hook with a skirt that cannot be pulled down the shank. These are very

Single hooks with skirting material added. MIKE TRETTIN

durable and will last quite a while as long as no teeth pierce that rubber band. I also use a bit of fly-tying Flashabou at times to give the trailer extra flash.

A native elder showed me a trick involving spoon trailers many years ago. We had been fishing that morning and had been quite successful, catching a great many pike and a few walleye for lunch. I was helping him clean the walleyes when he pulled out a piece of red yarn and rubbed it around in the juices and entrails of the walleyes. He then sealed it in a small plastic bag. Later that afternoon, we were fishing a large cabbage bed and after catching quite a few, the action started to slow down. The gentleman then pulled out the bag with the yarn, cut off a piece about three inches long, and instructed me to tie it on the rear split ring so that both ends trailed behind the spoon. The pike jumped all over it. I believe it was the addition of the walleye scent that made the difference, and I have used this trick successfully many times over the years.

Rattles

Lures with rattles are something of a mystery. There are times when pike can't leave them alone, and other times they don't want anything to do with them. However, there is one thing about rattlers that seems to hold up. They are far more effective in deeper water than they are in shallow. And darker days seem to make a difference, as does murky water. I draw this conclusion from watching how pike react to them in shallow water. Drag a rattler over the top of a pike in the shallows and it will spook many more times than not. There is a simple way to quiet those rattles, though, when you want to use a particular lure in shallow water.

I'll use one of my better crankbaits to illustrate this. The rattle chamber in a Magnum Bomber Long A is located in the head of the bait. Take a pair of pliers and hold a bent paperclip in its jaws. Hold the tag end of the clip over a heat source until it glows. Now, take this hot wire and bore a small hole into the rattle chamber. Put a small amount of cooking oil in a syringe and inject it into the chamber. Now reheat the clip and use it to smooth over the hole, sealing it. That cooking oil will quiet those rattles, and as long as not too much is used, it won't affect the action of the crankbait.

Glowing Lures

The question of color comes up quite often at seminars and on Web sites. Which color is best to use on pike? I've already covered this somewhat earlier in the book, but there is one aspect of color that I haven't mentioned, and that is the use of glowing lures. Once again, it is somewhat of a mystery. But, drawing on personal experience has enabled me to conclude a couple of facts concerning these glowing offerings.

First, the use of just a little glow has proven to be far more effective than using a lot of it. A lure that is totally glowing or one that is glowing too brightly seems to not only turn pike away, sometimes it seems to scare them. It is a case of "less is more" when it comes to using glowing offerings. Another discovery is that glowing lures seem to work best in dark conditions, like cloudy overcast days or in deep water. And this seems to hold up for the entire season, including fishing through the ice.

A couple of years ago, I took one of my good friends up to Nungesser Lake Lodge in northwest Ontario for the ice-out dead-bait bite. The ice went out early that year, and by the time we got there, the ice had been gone for six weeks. Normally, I would have been casting in the backs of bays by this time, but temperatures had remained low and the water temperatures were still around 46 degrees. It was a cold, dark, drizzly day when we set up on an incoming river where I had been successful in the past. We rigged up some dead suckers below floats. My friend had an Aqua-Vu camera along and we were glued to the screen. Time and time again we watched pike slowly nose up to the bait, but to my amazement, they would turn away without taking it. I had a couple of small glowing jig heads rigged with a trailing treble, and my friend decided to try one. It didn't take five minutes before his float tilted and he caught a nice one. So I tied on the other glowing jig and had the same results. The only difference from what we had been using was that little glowing jig head. I'm still scratching my head over that one, but I don't argue with success.

There are several ways to add just a bit of glow to your offerings. There are glowing paints on the market, which enable you to add just a touch to any lure. But the ones I have been most successful with, besides the jigs, are a grub and a skirted hook on spoons. There are several manufacturers that make glowing grubs, but if you charge up the entire grub, it may be just too much glow for the pike's liking. It is better to hold your hand over the grub, leaving about half of the tail exposed. By then shining a flashlight on this tip, it becomes supercharged. The rest of the body will have a kind of semi-glow, and the tip of the tail will really stand out. This works very well in thick cabbage.

The addition of just a few strands of glowing Flashabou, along with other colors, makes the skirted hook an effective tool to use on dark days. I believe it is best to charge up these glowing offerings before using them. There are several ways to accomplish this. There are several small lights on the market designed for this, or even an ordinary flashlight works fine. A camera flash will give them an intense glow.

CHAPTER TEN

Throwback Lures

Those of you who have fished for pike much have no doubt seen it. You are bringing in your lure, and there, directly behind your lure, an ominous dark shadow is closing in fast. You keep reeling, the hair on the back of your neck sticking straight out as it comes closer. Just as it gets fully into view, it stops and just hovers there, looking at you as though you said bad things about its mother. And then it turns and is gone. Quickly, you fire that lure back out there in the same vicinity and begin your retrieve. Whoa! Here she comes again, but this time as she gets close, she turns off without even giving you the evil eye.

This scenario, or some variation of it, is repeated anywhere people fish for pike. In this section of the book I want to share some of the tricks and tips we've learned to convert these followers into biters.

First, imagine a pike's head, especially its eyes. They sit on the top and to the sides of a pike's head. Now, stand straight up with your head straight and looking straight out in front. Without moving your head, look at your feet. Try as you might, all you can see are your own cheeks. The point I'm trying to illustrate here concerns the pike's field of view. If you look at a big pike's face, you'll see that they also have protruding cheeks, and can't look straight down any better than you can to see something close by. So while you are applying any triggering techniques, it is important to keep your lure either at the level of a pike's eyes or above it.

Think about the scene I described above. "Quickly, you fire that lure back out there in the same vicinity." That part is good, but the results may have been different if a different lure was thrown back. It is obvious you have the pike's attention because it followed. But something just wasn't right. Throwing back the same lure most times brings the same results until the pike loses interest. It is far better to give them something a bit different to look at. The change doesn't necessarily have to be huge. Something as subtle as a color change in the same lure might do it. Other times it may require a different lure with less or more action.

Here's a trick Mary and I learned by accident, but have used successfully many times since. Let's say I'm casting a crankbait and get a follow. If I spot the pike soon enough, and it is still a distance away from the boat, I'll stop the lure and let it float to the surface. The pike stops, too, and stares at the lure, transfixed. Mary then brings her lure, say an inline spinner, quickly past the pike. Wham! It seems that as the pike is lying there, if something close interrupts its concentration it will lash out at it. This trick works more often than not.

Another trick is one we call "the bait switch," and accounted for one of Mary's biggest pike at that time. We were experiencing a hot spoon bite and were catching lots of midsize pike, just having a ball. All of a sudden, along came grandma pike following Mary's spoon; then it stopped and turned away. I immediately traded rods with her, as mine had a different spoon on it. While she made her next cast, I changed the bait on her rod to a spoon the pike hadn't seen yet. She enticed the fish to follow again, but it didn't commit, and again turned away. Without taking her eyes off the fish, we traded rods again and Mary fired out another cast while I changed spoons again. We went through this bait switch a least a half-dozen times, and not once did Mary take her eyes off that fish, keeping its location marked. Finally, I hit on the right spoon and the pike jumped on it. Mary did a great job keeping her eye on the fish, and it paid off. My job was to switch the baits and put the new offering in her hand, while taking the used one away without getting the two rods tangled. This was teamwork at its finest.

There are probably some of you thinking, "Why didn't he cast to the fish?" We have a rule in our boat that a following fish belongs to the angler who brought it in, until he or she permits the other angler to cast to it. This eliminates hard feelings and makes nights in the cabin much more enjoyable. As with most things in life, I had to learn this through trial and error.

Whenever I'm in the boat, I always have a backup rod rigged. In the ideal situation of having enough room in the boat, I will have three rods rigged and ready. Two of them will be used for alternating lures, and the third will hold my backup. For instance, rod number one has a spoon on it. Rod number two has a spinnerbait, and the backup rod has a plastic lizard on it. I will alternate between the spoon and the spinnerbait, and will save the lizard for when I get a follow.

The idea is to throw something different back to them. It doesn't have to be a lizard, although it is one of my favorites. It could be a big tube bait like Lindy's Tiger Tube, or a big Slug-Go, or a Fin-S-Fish. These

Author's primary throwback lures: Slug-Go, jig-and-lizard, tube, jerkbait, and a Mepps spinner. JACK PENNY

are all subtle throwbacks; however, that is not always the best bet either. Sometimes a different spoon works, as in the above scenario. Or a spinner, or a crankbait. Different is the key. I usually have a soft plastic lure on to try first, but if the pike doesn't react and hit it, it will be something more aggressive on my next cast. Again, something different. Some of my favorite throwback lures are jig-and-lizard, Slug-Go, tube, jerkbait, and a Mepps spinner.

Throwing something different can pay off in a big way. We were on a river in northern Canada, watching two guys fishing off a rock at a place known as Bill's Island, named after the late, great Bill Tenney. (Bill's Island is a real hotspot and tons of huge pike have been caught there. It features a rock outcropping on the upstream side, which creates a large eddy below it.) They were casting spoons in the eddy. We watched as they caught several pike, but nothing big. We were fishing a spot nearby, and I kept an eye on these guys, expecting to see a monster landed any time. They kept casting those spoons and occasionally changing, but sticking with spoons. We must have watched them for an hour and a half, and all they threw were spoons.

When I saw them putting their gear into their boat, I fired up our motor; when they moved out, we moved in. Mary, armed with an inline spinner, and I with a spinnerbait, caught two pike over twenty pounds in about fifteen minutes, standing in the exact spot the other guys had occupied. The other two fishermen had motored out and were watching us. I could see their frustration as one started yelling at the other.

Casting something different was the key. Mary and I still chuckle over that one.

There are a couple of maneuvers that can be made that may eliminate the need to throw back. One is simply changing the direction of your retrieve. When you see a pike following, swing your rod to the side and give the reel several cranks. Then swing the rod to the other side and give it a few more cranks. Complete your retrieve, switching from side to side. This gives the appearance of something trying to escape and will often trigger a strike. Giving your lure any extra action while it is being followed is vastly better than just reeling it in so you can quickly make another cast. No matter what lure you have on, giving it a few jerks, or maybe a jerk and pause to flutter down, or changing the speed and direction, may be enough to trip the pike's trigger.

The other triggering maneuver is similar to the figure-eight maneuver that muskie anglers use, but with a couple of differences. When a pike follows all the way to boatside, you should make a 90-degree turn in one direction with at least a rod's length of line out. Unlike the muskie men, however, do not stick your rod in the water. Instead, just lead the lure along the side of the boat, and make a wide turn to bring it back down the same path. The percentage of fish that will fall for this trick is not high, but it is better than not trying at all. And when they do hit, it is an explosion, resulting in true, exciting, toe-to-toe combat.

CHAPTER ELEVEN

Table Fare

While I am a strong proponent of releasing all large pike, this does not mean that I release all pike. In waters with a sustainable population of pike, there is nothing wrong with removing a few small pike for table fare. The fact of the matter is, pike are excellent eating fish. They can be fried, baked, poached, boiled, and even pickled, all with great results.

While fishing in some of the less-populated regions, shore lunch is usually a daily ritual for us. Depending on where we are and the conditions outside, we either build a small fire or use a Coleman propane stove. If you decide to build a fire, for safety's sake don't do it on wet rocks. Steam can build up in wet rocks and they sometimes explode, showering everyone nearby with burning embers and rock shards. Also, make sure to fully douse your fire with water whenever you are finished.

There are a few ways to clean and prepare a pike for cooking. I prefer to eat pike with as few bones as possible, so I fillet mine.

How to Fillet a Northern Pike

1. Hold the pike by grasping it by the gills and lay it on its back. Insert the point of the knife in the soft area between the gills and ahead of the pectoral fins.

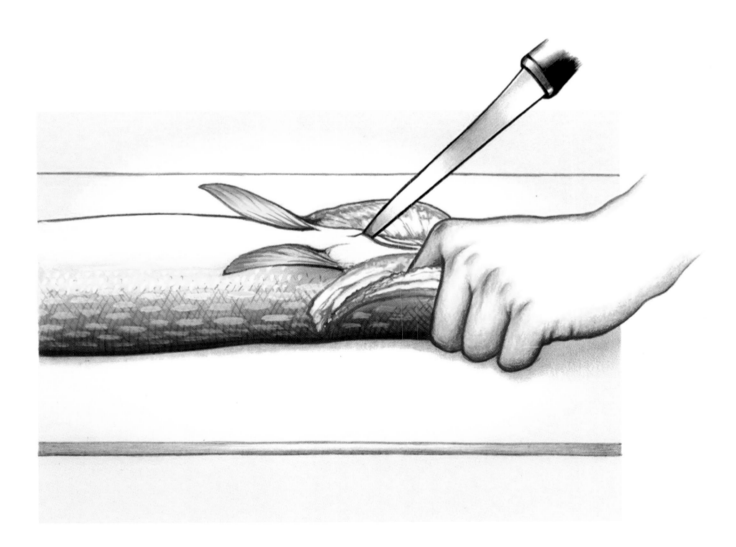

2. Make the initial cut down the middle toward the tail, keeping between the two pelvic fins, and stop by the anal fin in front of the tail.

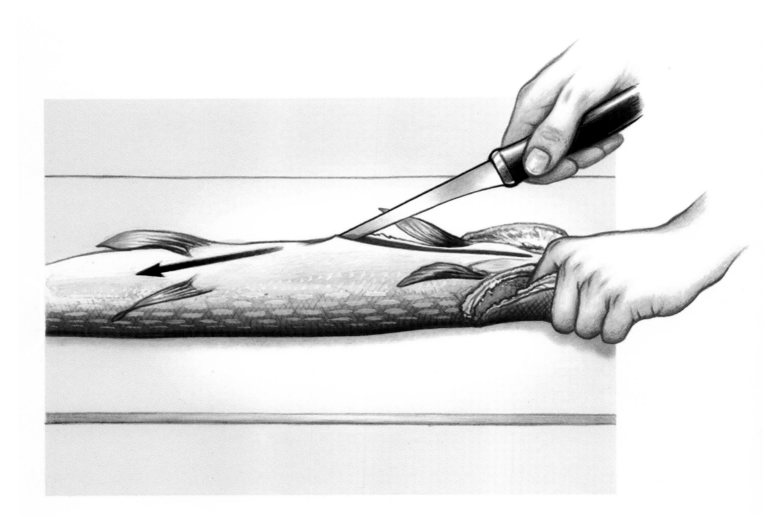

3. Lay the pike on its side and make a cut just behind the gills down to the backbone. Be careful not to cut completely through the backbone.

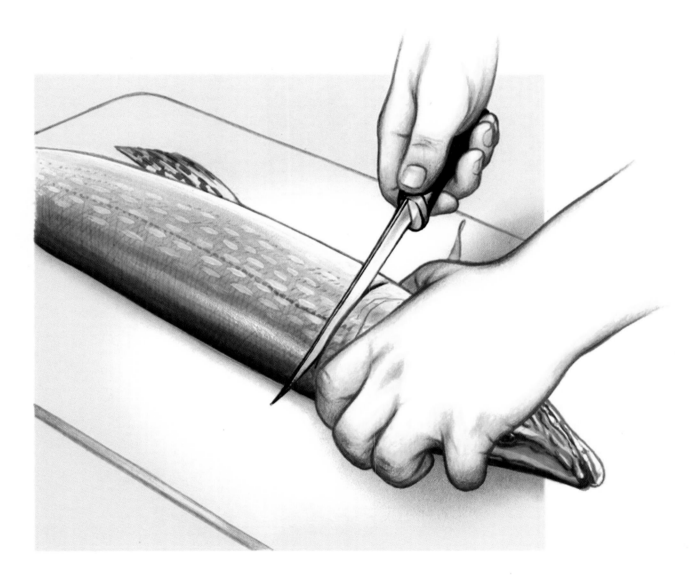

4. Turn the knife sideways so that the blade's grind runs alongside the backbone, and saw along that bone to the tail. You will hear the blade cutting through ribs and Y-bones. Make the cut completely to the tail and out through the skin. Remove the fillet and repeat the process on the other side. You now have two slabs of meat with skin and bones intact.

5. The next step is the removal of the fins. This is easily done by grasping the fin, holding it up, and slicing underneath it.

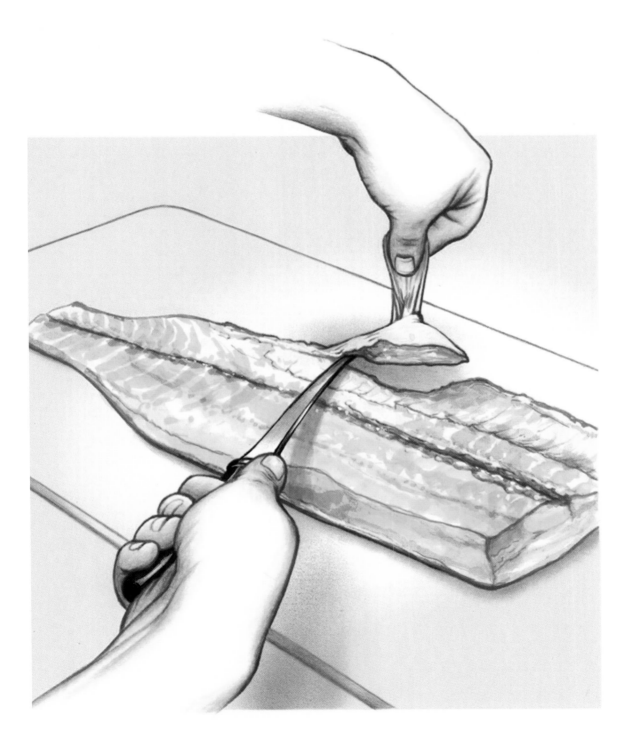

6. Time to get rid of those ribs, which you can feel with your fingers. Find where they start and make a cut just behind them. As you cut deeper, turn the knife blade slightly upward to keep in contact with the bones, while you make long slices down the row of ribs.

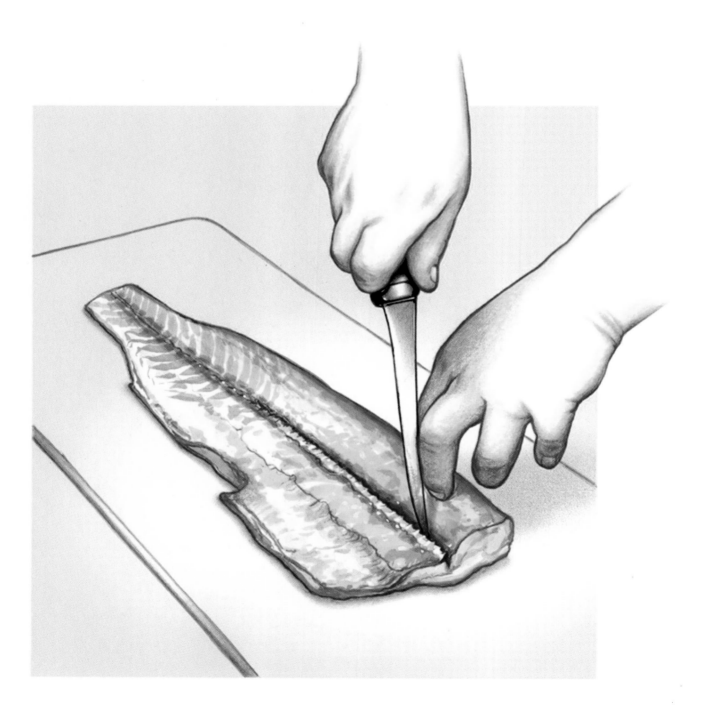

Removing the Y-Bones

At this point, the ribs have been removed from our fillets, but the skin is still intact. Looking at the fillet, you will see a line running down the middle of the meat, and with closer inspection, a row of white dots about a half-inch above it. If you don't see these white dots, run your fingers along the length and you will feel them. The line is the lateral line, and those white spots are the ends of the Y-bones. After locating them, take your fillet knife and make a cut about a half-inch deep on the outside of the bone tips, down the length of the fillet to the spot where the anal fin was.

Next, insert the tip of the blade at the start of the lateral line, about a half-inch deep, and make a cut the same length as before. Now go back to the first cut above the Y-bones and angle the knife blade toward the top part of the fillet (the thicker part). Slice down, following the bones, about a half to three-quarters of an inch deep, and make the cut following the previous one there.

Go back to the lateral-line cut and again angle the blade to follow the bones. Make this cut, following the previous one, just deep enough to reach the end of the bones.

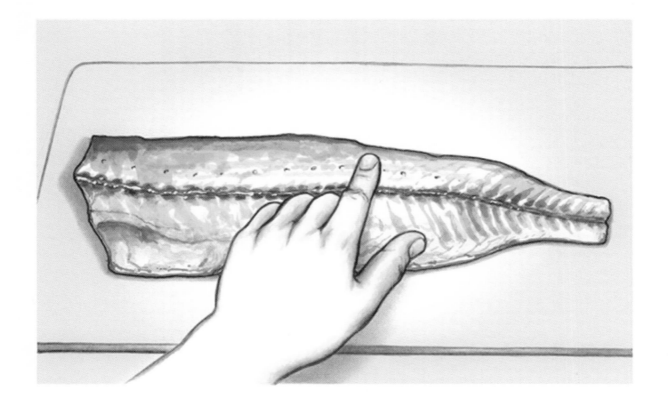

Once you have completed this cut down the length of the fillet, you should be able to grasp the strip of meat between the two cuts and pull it away from the fillet.

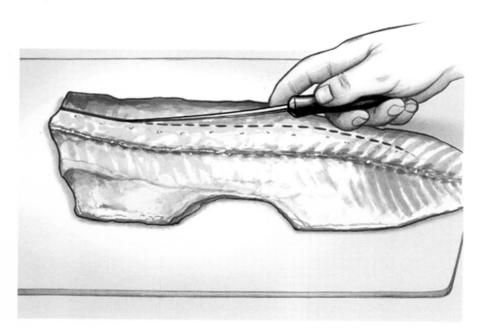

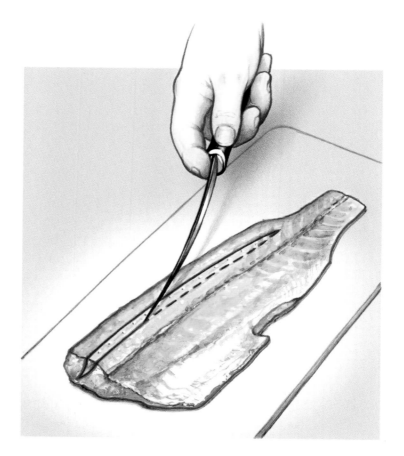

Now it is time to remove the skin. You will need to grasp the tail end tightly. A pair of pliers is a great help for this process. Grip the end of the tail and cut into the flesh while turning the blade flat; using a sawing motion, cut close to the skin. It helps a lot to jerk the pliers hand back and forth, pulling sideways while sawing with the other hand. Make the cut completely down the length of the fillet and remove the skin.

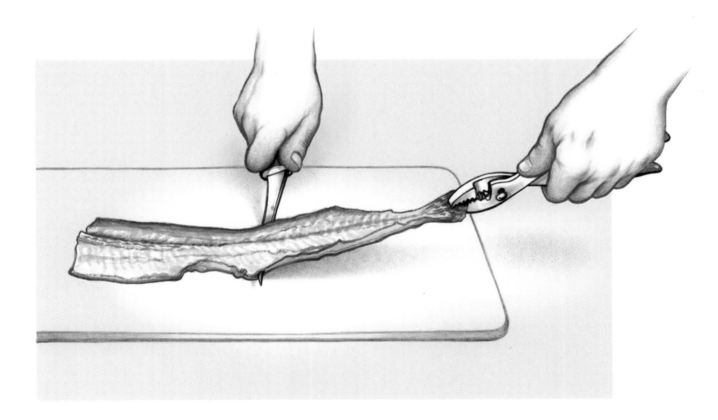

Frying Pike

Now that you have successfully filleted your fish, it is time to fry it up. First, the fillets need to be washed off and patted dry with a paper towel. It can be cooked in one piece, but with the strip of meat containing the Y-bones removed, it has different thicknesses and will fry better if cut into smaller, bite-sized pieces.

I like to dust the pieces with flour, and then dip them in a mixture of egg and milk. I coat the outside with a 50/50 mixture of flour and ground-up cornflakes. This gives the fish a crunchy coating on the outside. You can add different spices to suit your personal taste. I like to use seasoned salt, lemon pepper, and a touch of garlic. A Cajun mixture is also very tasty. This is a good time to experiment.

Make sure your oil is very hot before adding the fish. A small amount of coating or flour dropped into it will start to sizzle right away if it's ready. If you are frying a larger piece, be sure to place the fish in the pan skin-side down initially, to prevent the ends from curling up. (The skin side will be the flat, smooth side.) Cook until golden brown, then flip once to cook the other side. The meat should be flaky when done.

CHAPTER TWELVE

Education

To consistently be one of the pike anglers who, more times than not, catches giant pike, you have to do the homework that's involved. I cannot stress enough the importance of gathering information. After all, knowledge is the key to success and the more you know, the better your results will be.

Big fish are rarely easy. Yes, there will always be those chance encounters, and Lady Luck seems to play a part occasionally. But more often, doing one's homework will produce much more in the long run.

Most anglers would like to consistently catch the kind of big fish that guys like Jack Burns, Bill Tenney, Rob Kimm, Doug Stange, or Jan Eggers do. But these guys were not born under a lucky star, nor do they just have luck on their side. They all continually do their homework on the water, and they all use past experiences as lessons learned. This is important. When you are on the water and catch a good one, take note of details around you. As years roll by and you get more experienced, if you can recall these bits of knowledge you can reapply them. Without exception, all really top anglers, regardless of what species they are targeting, notice these things and remember them for future use.

Learn from others in the know, and retain the lessons they teach. Take notes, and stash them in your tackle box if you need to. Read everything you can find on the subject, and spend as much time as possible with experienced anglers, like guides.

For those who don't have an opportunity to spend vast amounts of time on the water, this is a chance to benefit from those who do. Guides are a great bargain if you learn from them. If you take a trip with a guide, pick his brain. He is there to educate you. If the guide is fishing too, study how he works each lure. When you are fishing a piece of structure, watch where he casts and ask him why he cast there. And pay attention to where and how he positions his boat. In general, ask questions about everything and anything. Learn all you can from your guide.

Read everything you can lay your hands on. Not only on pike, but also on any forage fish they consume. If you know the habits of a pike's prey, you will know the habits of pike. This book is a good start, but don't stop here. By reading what others write, you have the benefit of not only learning what has been most successful for me, but what others have experienced as well. Books, magazines, videos, and television are all great learning tools.

Esox Angler magazine is one good choice. It is partnered with *The Next Bite* television show, which features informative shows on pike each season. The *In-Fisherman* is another great multimedia group with lots of valuable information, and its techniques book on pike is a must-read for anybody interested in the species. It also has a wonderful video library with several videos on pike, along with continued coverage of northerns in their magazine and television show.

In closing, become a student of pike and do your homework. It will pay off in the end.

INDEX

B

bait, 43–45

    and ice fishing, 92–94, 95–96

    and quick-strike rigs, 41–42

bays. *See* lakes

beaver structures, 61–62

Blue Fox Vibrax. *See also* lures, 68

Bomber Magnum Long A's. *See also* lures, 71, 104

bucktail jigs. See also jigs, 80–81

Burns, Jack, 123

Burt (lure). *See also* jerkbaits, 69, 79, 80

C

cabbage (*Potamogeton amplifolius*). *See also* weeds, 67–68

cameras, underwater, 87–88

casting gear, 23–25

Cop-E-Cat spoon. *See also* spoons, 64, 65

cradles, 8, 9, 10–11

crankbaits. *See also* lures

    in rivers, 75, 84

    in rocky areas, 71, 72–73, 81

    in spring, 52–53, 58

    in summer, 64

D

dams. *See* beaver structures

Dardevle lure. *See also* lures, 55, 102

dens. *See* beaver structures

depth finders, 27, 87

E

Eddie Bait (lure). *See also* jerkbaits, 78, 79

Eggers, Jan, 41, 123

electronic equipment, 27–28

equipment. *See also* hooks; lures, 8–11, 21–39

electronics, 27–28

    hook files, 26–27

    for ice fishing, 87–88, 91–92

    landing devices, 8–9

    leaders, 28–39

    lines, 24

    for removing hooks, 11–12

    rods and reels, 21–26

    sunglasses, 28

    for trolling, 74

Esox Angler (magazine), 124

Esox Cobra Jig. *See also* jigs, 80, 81

F

fall fishing, 77–84

    near rocks, 81–82

    in rivers, 82, 84

    in weeds, 77–81

files, hook, 26–27

fishing. See pike fishing

Fittante, Joe, 18

forage fish, 43–44, 89–90

    in beaver structures, 61

    learning about, 124

G

gliders. *See also* jerkbaits, 78–79

GPS (Global Positioning System) units, 27–28, 87

guides, fishing, 124

H

Haywire Twist Tool, 36

hooks

    changing, 102, 103

    files for, 26–27

    and quick-strike rigs, 41–43, 44, 45–46, 92, 95

    removing, 11–14

I

ice fishing, 85–99

    bait for, 92–94

    equipment for, 87–88, 91–92

    locating fish, 88–90

    safety, 85–86

    setting up, 94–96

    thickness of ice, 86–87

    tips for, 96–99

In-Fisherman (magazine), 3, 41, 124

inline spinners. *See also* lures

    in rivers, 76, 84

    in spring, 51–52

    in weeds, 68

J

jaw spreaders, 11–12, 13, 14

jerkbaits. *See also* lures, 24–25, 26

in fall weeds, 78–80

near beaver structures, 62

in summer weeds, 69–70

jigs. *See also* lures

drift jigging, 73–74

in fall weeds, 80–81

in rivers, 76

in spring, 54–55

in summer weeds, 68–69

Johnson Silver Minnow spoon.
See also spoons, 52, 55, 102

K

Kimm, Rob, 123

Kit-A-Mat spoon. *See also* spoons,
64, 65

Knipex hook cutters, 11–12, 14

Kwik Kradle, 8, 9, 11

L

lakes

bays in summer, 63–66

ice fishing on, 88–99

rocky areas in summer, 70–74

spawning bays and potholes,
46–47

spring locations and lures for,
49–59

trolling breaklines in
summer, 74

weeds in fall, 77–81

weeds in summer, 66–70

landing devices, 8–9

and removing hooks, 11

using, 10–11

Lax, Rick, 17

Lax, Ron, 17

leaders, 28–39

fluorocarbon, 29

for ice fishing, 92

making, 29–39

lines, weight of, 24

lizards. *See also* jigs, 68–69

lures. *See also* specific types of

alternating, 107–11

for bays in summer, 63,
64–65, 66

for fall rivers, 82–84

for fall weeds, 78–81

glowing, 105–6

for lakes in spring, 50–56

and leaders, 28, 29

modifications to, 101–4

near beaver structures, 62

with rattles, 104

and reels, 25–26

for rocky areas, 71–74,
81–82

for spring rivers, 59–60

for summer rivers, 75–76

for summer weeds, 66–70

trolling breaklines, 74

and water clarity, 56–58

M

Magic Maker. *See also* jerkbaits,
78, 79

Mepps Muskie Magnum. *See also*
lures, 68

mounts. *See* reproduction mounts

N

nets, long-handled, 9, 11

Next Bite, The (television), 124

northern pike. *See also* pike
fishing

aggressiveness of, 1, 2

field of vision, 107–8

filleting, 112–18

frying, 121–22

hearing of, 55

preserving species, 7–8,
19–20, 45–46

removing Y-bones, 119–21

seasonal movements of, 5–6

spawning, 40, 46

P

perch. *See also* forage
fish, 61, 89

pike. *See* northern pike

pike fishing. *See also* specific
seasons; equipment

catch-and-release, 7–8

landing devices, 8–9

landing methods, 9–11

learning, 123–24

photographing fish, 14–15,
19

quick-strike rigs, 41–46

releasing fish, 15–16, 17

removing hooks, 11–14

reproduction mounts, 16–18

weighing fish, 15

pliers, needle-nose, 11–12

prey fish. *See* forage fish

Q

quick-strike rigs, 41–46

and ice fishing, 91, 92, 95–96

R

Rapala Husky Jerk. *See also* lures, 53

Real Image spoon. *See also* spoons, 64, 65

reels. *See also* rods, 25–26

    for gliders, 79

    for ice fishing, 91

    for spoons, 55–56

reproduction mounts, 16–18

resources, 124

rigs. *See* quick-strike rigs

rivers

    in fall, 82, 84

    during spawning, 48

    in spring, 59–60

    in summer, 75–76

    in winter, 99–100

rocks

    in fall, 81–82

    in summer, 70–74

rod-and-reel combinations. *See* rods; reels

rods, 21–25

    casting gear, 23–25

    spinning gear, 21–22, 22–23

S

sinkers. *See also* lures, 41, 92

spear fishing. *See also* ice fishing, 85

spinnerbaits. *See also* lures, 26

    in cabbage, 68, 69

    in fall rivers, 84

    in fall weeds, 78

    in spring, 58, 62

    in summer, 64

spinning gear, 21–22, 22–23, 25

spoons. *See also* lures, 25–26

    in fall rivers, 84

    in fall weeds, 78

    modifications to, 101–4

    in spring, 55–56

    in summer, 64, 65, 72

    and water clarity, 58

    weedless, 52, 53, 62, 66–67, 68

spring fishing, 49–60

    in lakes, 49–59

    near beaver structures, 61–62

    in rivers, 59–60

Squirrely Burt. *See also* jerkbaits, 69, 80

Squirrely Jake. *See also* lures, 71, 72

Stalkers. *See also* lures, 71, 72, 81–82

Stange, Doug, 123

structures. *See* beaver structures

Suick. *See also* lures, 69, 79, 80

summer fishing, 63–76

    in lake bays, 63–66

    in rivers, 75–76

    in rocky areas, 70–74

    trolling breaklines, 74

    in weeds, 66–70

sunglasses, 28

Super Shad Raps. *See also* lures, 64, 66, 81

swimbaits. *See also* lures, 60, 61

T

tackle. *See* equipment

Tenney, Bill, 110, 123

tools. *See* equipment

topwater lures. *See also* lures, 50–51, 52

trolling. *See also* pike fishing, 24, 72, 74

trophies. *See* reproduction mounts

W

walleyes, 59, 72

water lilies. *See also* weeds, 66–67

water temperature. *See also* specific seasons

    and movements, 5–6

    when spawning, 40, 46–47

weather. *See* water temperature

weeds

    in fall, 77–81

    in summer, 66–70

    in winter, 90

weigh sack, 15

winter fishing. *See also* ice fishing, 99–100

Jack Penny grew up in the Midwest during the 1950s. He gained a love of the outdoors by hunting and fishing with his father, Ward. The values instilled in him at that time stayed with him throughout his teens and into adulthood. After his first trip to Canada in the mid-70s with some friends, Jack made the decision to focus his energies on northern pike. He started spending most of his free time gathering as much information about these fish as he could and fishing for them whenever time allowed. He became obsessed with learning everything he could and applying it on the water. The knowledge he gained eventually landed him eight world line-class records and more memories than one can count.

MARY PENNY

He has fished in the northern United States as well as six Canadian provinces and across Alaska. He writes for several outdoor magazines and is currently a staff writer and regular contributor for *Esox Angler* magazine.

His quest for knowledge hasn't stopped here. He still attempts to absorb any and all information that is available, which he maintains is the key to his success. His wife, Mary, travels regularly with him, as they share their love of the great outdoors together. They have one daughter, Janelle, who also enjoys time on the water with her parents.